The World
Of Model Trains

The World

Of Model Trains

Guy R. Williams

G. P. PUTNAM'S SONS

NEW YORK

This book was designed and produced by
Rainbird Reference Books Limited
Marble Arch House, 44 Edgware Road, London, W2,
for G. P. Putnam's Sons Limited,
200 Madison Avenue, New York, N.Y. 10016

House Editor: Peter Coxhead

Designer: Gwyn Lewis

Library of Congress Catalog Card Number 79–114165

Published simultaneously in the
Dominion of Canada by
Longmans Canada Limited, Toronto

The text was set in Monophoto Imprint 11/13 by
Jolly & Barber Limited, Rugby, England
The book was printed and bound by
Dai Nippon Printing Company Limited,
Tokyo, Japan

PRINTED IN JAPAN

Contents

List of Color Plates

Acknowledgments

No book of this kind, dealing with so wide-ranging a subject, could be compiled without much assistance from the recognised authorities. Among those to whom I am especially grateful are the following people and companies who have contributed significantly to the material contained in the book, or who have most generously given information or advice, or have helped in other ways. Nevertheless, full editorial responsibility for the text and for the captions to the pictures is my own.

Australia

Rupert J. Ackland: Acting State Secretary, Australian Model Railway Association, New South Wales Branch.
Ken Elder: President, Melbourne Model Railway Society.
C. B. Gilbertson: Assistant Secretary, Australian Model Railway Association, New South Wales Branch.
Rex Little: Federal Secretary, Australian Model Railway Association.

Belgium

Georges Desbarax: President, MOROP (Verband Modellbahn Europa).

France

J. L. Fournereau: Editor, *Loco-Revue*.
Henri Girod-Eymery: Muséon di Rodo, Uzès.

Germany

Fleischmann Brothers: Nuremberg.
Märklin Brothers: Göppingen, Württemberg.

Great Britain

John Anning: Chairman, The Model Railway Club.
Ron Bailey: Anglia Film Productions.
Bassett-Lowke (Northampton) Limited.
Lt. Col. Beattie: Beatties of London.
Donald Boreham: Author, *Narrow Gauge Railway Modelling*.
H. F. Bower: Honorary Secretary, The Gauge O Guild.
British Trix Limited, Wrexham, Denbighshire.

Keith Capon: Past President, National Model Railroad Association (British Region).
W. A. Carter: Honorary Secretary, The Society of Model and Experimental Engineers.
Roye England: The Pendon Museum Trust.
R. T. Everett: Librarian, Institution of Mechanical Engineers, London.
Cyril J. Freezer: Editor, *Railway Modeller*.
Gordon Heywood: Exhibition Manager, Historical Model Railway Society.
David Jenkinson: Author, *Locomotive Liveries of the L.M.S.*
D. L. Kearsey: The Pendon Museum Trust.
H. George McGhee: President, National Model Railroad Association, (British Region).
Pritchard Patent Products Company: Seaton, Devon.
S. J. Roberts: Secretary, The Gauge 1 Model Railway Society.
Rovex Industries Limited: Margate, Kent.
H. M. Sell: Late Manager, Messrs Bassett-Lowke's London Showroom.
J. N. Slinn: Honorary Secretary, The Historical Model Railway Society.
Paul Towers: Late Editor, *Model Railway News*.
R. H. Vivian: Honorary Secretary, The 2mm Scale Association.
Trevor Wilkinson: Crawley, Sussex.
R. Wills: Managing Director, Industrial Display Co. Ltd.
C. R. Wrenn: Managing Director, G. and R. Wrenn Ltd.

Italy

Ottorino Bisazza: President, Lima, Vicenza.
Rivarossi SpA: Como.

New Zealand

Maurice Duston: President, New Zealand Model Railway Guild (Inc).

Switzerland

I. A. Wismann: Librarian, The Swiss Institute of Transport and Communications, Lucerne.

United States of America

Bill McClanahan: The Dallas Morning News.
Roger H. Poindexter: Sales Manager, Tyco Industries Inc.
Whit Towers: President, National Model Railroad Association.
Linn H. Westcott: Editor, *Model Railroader*.

Glossary

Some of the words and phrases used in this book may need a little explanation. Others are used in different ways by railway modellers on the two sides of the Atlantic Ocean. Even the primary name given to the prototype varies between 'Railway' (in Britain and most other English-speaking countries) and 'Railroad' (in America). These notes may help to lessen the confusion:

Ballast: Hard, granular material used to keep sleepers UK and ties USA in position.

Bogie UK – **Truck** USA: An under-carriage attached to a locomotive or car that is free to swivel so that curves may be turned.

Bolster: The principal cross-member of a bogey or truck.

Caboose USA: A car found normally at the rear of an American freight train.

Carriage UK – **Coach** USA.

Catenary: A system of overhead wires used in many electrified railways.

Chairs: Fittings fastened to cross-track sleepers or ties for securely holding the rails.

Concertina Connection: Flexible passage-way between two carriages UK or coaches USA.

Conductor USA – **Guard** UK.

Double-acting Cylinder: A cylinder into which steam is introduced to return as well as to propel the piston.

Engine Driver UK – **Engineer** US.

Flat Wagons UK – **Flatcars** USA: Freight cars that are merely flat platforms on wheels. They are used for the transportation of standardized containers.

Foot-plate UK: A vantage point from which an engine driver and his assistant can survey the track ahead.

Freight Car USA – **Goods Wagon** or **Truck** UK.

Freight Train USA – **Goods Train** UK.

Frog: A component formed when rails join or cross.

Ganger: A man responsible for the upkeep of track.

Gauge: The word used to establish the track width of a prototype or a model in relation to all other track widths.

Gondola Car USA: A railroad car having a platform body with low sides.

Goods Train *see* Freight Train.

Guard *see* Conductor.

Guard's Van UK – **Caboose** USA, which see.

Hessian: Material that resembles sacking.

Interlocking Tower USA – **Signal Box** UK.

Livery: The surface markings applied to trains and their various component parts.

Pantograph: 1. A mechanical device used in the production of moulds for scale models. 2. An articulated fitting used with an overhead electrified line.

Parades: Paved surfaces provided for the convenience of waiting passengers in the early railways.

Passenger Carriages UK – **Passenger Coaches** USA.

Pilot Truck: The bogey UK or truck USA that precedes the driving wheels.

Points UK – **Switches** or **Turnouts** USA.

Rack Engine UK – **Cog Engine** USA: An engine which has a geared spur wheel that engages with the indentations in a specially prepared rail, for security purposes.

Railroad Car USA – **Railway Wagon** UK.

Rakes: Sets of similar carriages UK or coaches USA.

Rolling Stock: The locomotives, cars and other vehicles used on a railway or railroad.

Shunting UK – **Switching** USA.

Shunting Engine UK – **Switcher** USA.

Signal Box *see* Interlocking Tower.

Signalman UK – **Towerman** USA.

Sleepers UK – **Ties** or **Crossties** USA: The transverse supports on which rails are fastened to keep them in line.

Stud: 1. A small piece of metal projecting from the surface of a model railway track used for completing an electric circuit. 2. A collection of locomotives.

Switcher USA – **Shunting Engine** UK.

Tappet Interlocking Mechanism: A device in which sliding rods or bars engage with others, to prevent unwanted movement (as for example, of signals).

Tender: A car or carriage, separate from a locomotive but connected to it, that is used for transporting fuel and water.

Toothed Rack *see* Rack Engine.

Towerman *see* Signalman.

Truck UK – **Freight Car** USA.

Turnouts *see* Points.

Wagon UK *see* Railroad Car.

Wagon-ways: The primitive installations, used for transporting ore and other basic materials, from which railways UK and railroads USA eventually developed.

1 The World of Model Railways

A small crowd gathers, and the members of it look intently at a beautiful miniature landscape lit from a radiant blue sky. There are men, women and children in the crowd – the youngest standing on long footstools that raise them to a suitable viewing level. The attention of every person present is centred on a small replica of a viaduct, with stone piers and an intricate superstructure of thin timber beams. This carries a pair of shining nickel steel rails over the valley between two scrub-covered hills. Near one end of the viaduct, model trees as large (or as small) as rock-garden plants provide a fresh green frame for the entrance of a tunnel.

Then, with a soft purr of wheels, a tiny train emerges from the tunnel. The locomotive, barely as long as two fingers, draws four truly proportioned coaches in slow procession to a point a little more than half-way across the viaduct, then – controlled by an unseen hand – the little train slows gradually to a halt so that the admiring viewers can examine it closely.

Each person, one can be certain, will look at the stationary engine and coaches in a different way.

All the people in the crowd who have ever used their hands to make anything more precise than a batter pudding will be fascinated by the technical perfection of the models.

The men in the crowd, especially those who have been involved in the world-wide Do-it-Yourself movement, will wonder at the amount of almost microscopic detail that has been incorporated in the locomotive and the coaches by highly skilled craftsmen. Each model is the result of some hundreds of hours of preparatory work. The labourers have toiled for the sheer pleasure their cleverness has brought them. If they had charged their time against the cost of the enterprise, the layout would be virtually priceless.

The women, by nature more interested in domesticity and comfort, will be peering through the windows of the coaches at the passengers, shorter than match-sticks but complete in every detail, who sit on the minute, exquisitely upholstered seats.

The children in the crowd may not be thinking of the models as models at all. With the capacity for make-believe that is shared by all young people, they will be gazing with wide eyes at a real train

1 A scene which can be duplicated throughout the world – enthusiasts at a model train exhibition.

13

Above left – A small part of the Alturas and Lone Pine layout constructed by Whitney K. Towers.

Left – A Great Western Railway train leaving the tunnel and crossing the balsawood viaduct in the Pendon layout. The original viaduct was 132 feet high and just over 1,000 feet long – the model viaduct is 3 feet 6 inches long and made of 4,686 pieces.

Above – Layouts can be easily made from commercial sources.

Right – Model trains are always a great success at international toy fairs. Here is one being enthusiastically studied at Nuremberg.

that has stopped on a real viaduct in a wholly private country to enter which they alone have the necessary passports and visas. When that little train starts again, each of the children will, in his or her imagination, be driving it.

The young man at the unobtrusively placed control panel who has brought the train to a halt will have been watching with mixed feelings of pleasure and responsibility. It is his task to make the trains that use the viaduct stop and start and move at a convincing speed – scale speed – and it is his job, too, to keep them going, by skill and will power, even though the chance of a mechanical breakdown – always to be feared on miniature layouts – is increased by the presence of visitors.

All, from the smallest child to the hoariest grandfather there, will have fallen victim to a more or less marked extent to the magic of model railways.

This is a magic that knows no national boundaries. Model railways run, and are loved, in almost every corner of the world. In terms of popularity, railway modelling does not fall far behind such universal favourites as fishing and football.

In Britain, where railways originated, more than fifty clubs and societies formed by model enthusiasts are affiliated to the Model Railway Club, the central organization. Many of these subsidiary bodies have an international membership. The National Model Railroad Association, the principal American body, besides acting as the main link between enthusiasts all over the United States, has a thriving branch in Britain. MOROP (Model Verband Europ – the European model railway union, the body that co-ordinates the activities of the railway modellers of most of the countries of that continent) attempts to define standards for at least two hundred thousand associates. There are railway model lovers who are gregarious enough to cohere into clubs and societies in Austria, Australia, Belgium, Canada, Denmark, France, Germany, Hungary, Italy, Japan, The Netherlands, New Zealand, Spain, Sweden and Switzerland, and small isolated groups in many other countries.

Undoubtedly, it is the marked sociability of the people who love model railways that attracts a steady flow of new members to these organizations. It would be hard to find any friendlier body of men than the officials and members of the average model railway club or society. They help each other cheerfully, without expecting any return. They provide information even before it is asked for. They hold clinics, or technical advice sessions, lectures and slide show presentations, for free. They correspond with members of the fraternity in other countries as though national boundaries do not even exist. They travel long distances – even, overseas – to conventions. (When a party of American railroad enthusiasts recently stopped off in Australia, during a 'steam fan' tour of the Southern

A detail of the model of the 2–2–0 Planet in the Science Museum London; the prototype was built in 1830 by Stephenson & Co. for the Liverpool and Manchester Railway

Pacific, members of the Australian Railway Historical Association chartered a train specially to take them on a sight-seeing trip. That is typical of the spirit of kindness and hospitality encountered everywhere in the world of model railways. Compared to railway modellers, the accredited members of some of the world's well-known religious bodies seem self-centred and prim.)

When any hobby becomes extremely popular, it inevitably attracts the attention of charitably minded people who are eager to cater for the needs of the enthusiasts and, incidentally, are not unwilling to make an honest penny, or nickel, or two in the process. The great German model-producing firms export their splendid wares to no fewer than fifty countries. The new Italian firms are quite as successful. Japanese-made miniature locomotives are collected just as keenly in North and South America as they are in Europe and Australasia. In the United States alone, at least ten million dollars' worth of model railroad equipment is sold every year.

With the production and consumption of railway models running at these very high levels, there will inevitably be waste. The fact that within two years a high proportion of the models sold will be lying neglected and forgotten in junk rooms and cupboards may seem a little shocking. But even these discarded playthings will have served some useful purpose, for they will have brought a new richness into the lives of many people who may be too restless and dynamic to concentrate on any one pastime for long.

Probably, too, much of the equipment will have been bought for, used by, and then put aside by, children and young people. If this is the case, it will have fully justified its existence. In the words of Linn H. Westcott, Editor of the magazine *Model Railroader* :

'Despite its brief period of use, the toy train is one of the best things a child can appreciate at a certain period in his life. There is hardly a better way to provide the experiences of putting things together in various combinations; of learning about the action and timing of motor-powered machinery; of becoming acquainted with some of the benefits and nuisances of electrical circuitry; of simulating a part of the industrial world in miniature . . .'

But when the child becomes a man, should he not put away childish things, as he is so often urged to do?

To the unconverted, there may be something rather amusing or even ridiculous about the sight of adults – mature, responsible adults – playing with children's toys or what appear to be children's toys. But railway modelling appeals to the fully grown for quite legitimate reasons that are not difficult to understand.

scene on J. Lawton's Gauge TT
ansmoor Central layout.

6 Above – Walter Harper has his
own museum. The model close to hi
is of a South Eastern and Chathe
well tank, made about 1860.

7 Left – An old craftsman makes
a few final adjustments to a mode
of the Stephensons' Rocket.

8 Above right – two fine scale
Gauge O models. Top, a London
and North Western Railway
0–6–0 saddle tank engine (1870)
modelled by J. S. Beeson in 195
powered by an electric engine.
Below, the 4–4–0 Quantock, one
of the Great Western Railway's
'Duke' class (1897).

9 Right – King's-Canterbury, or
of the Southern Railway's 4–4–0
'Schools' Class, modelled by F.
Tucker. This is live steam and bu
to $3\frac{1}{2}$ in. gauge.

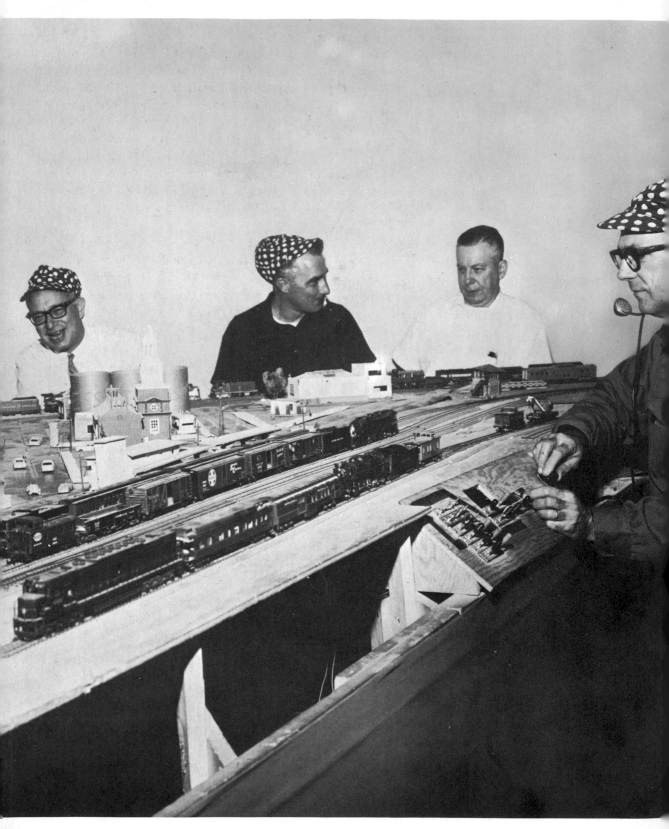

Many adults who are attracted to the hobby could just as easily become collectors of antique furniture, or fine silver, or Impressionist paintings, or netsuke, or any other objects of beauty and value. Enthusiasts of this kind get acute pleasure from looking at, and handling, examples of splendid craftsmanship, and they get extra satisfaction from actually owning the objects of their admiration. Periodically, sales of the most exquisite railway models are held in the great auction rooms of the world. Competition on these occasions is fierce, and prices are high. In some countries, gangs of thieves have discovered that railway models are almost as worth taking as gold, or diamonds, from the houses and flats they make the subjects of their raids.

Other people become model railway addicts because the models they buy or make reproduce in miniature a form of transport that they find particularly fascinating. For more than a century and a half, trains have intrigued a large proportion of the population – both adult and juvenile – of every country in which they run. It is hardly surprising that this affection spills over to include the replicas of the best-loved prototypes.

But healthy and active adults and children are not the only people to whom railway modelling commends itself. Physicians, surgeons and physiotherapists have been quick to see the value of the hobby as a healing aid. After the Second World War, model building was encouraged in many hospitals as an ancillary activity. By being taught to acquire the simplest skills, servicemen who had been badly wounded in the war could be helped to regain the use of their hands. The model railways produced by these handicapped veterans under expert supervision provided benefit and spiritual distraction for themselves. The Gowanda State Hospital, Helmuth, New York, is one of several institutions in which the possibilities of these post-war therapeutic experiments were further explored.

Occasionally, model railways are used for more extraordinary purposes.

There is, for instance, one American psychiatrist who uses miniature railroads for helping his patients to sort out their marital difficulties. In his consulting rooms he has had installed twin HO Gauge layouts. Each time a husband and wife take him their intimate problems, he encourages his visitors to operate the layouts, placing one of the partners of the marriage at each set of controls. The layouts are planned in such a way that if the two operators are in complete harmony the train movements will be synchronized. From the way in which the patients fail to synchronize the movements of the trains – if they do fail – the psychiatrist claims to be able to diagnose what is wrong with their relationship.

Model railways are not always playthings. This psychiatrist charges a substantial fee.

Operating model trains has therapeutic value and at least one hospital uses a model train layout for the treatment of badly wounded war veterans.

2 How Railways Began

It will be shown, a little later in this book, that the history of railway modelling is almost as long and as detailed as that of the railways themselves. Miniature replicas of the earliest locomotives and coaches were being produced even before the prototypes had had a chance to lose their first freshness. So, the book must start at the very beginning if it is to give as complete a picture as possible of the world of model railways.

The first moving, man-made containers that could (at a pinch) be called railway wagons were the rough trucks that were used for transporting ore, in the German and Rumanian mines during the sixteenth century. The trucks, which ran on smooth wooden rails, had wooden wheels. These wheels had crude flanges that prevented the trucks from running off the rails. The basic principle of railway safety had been discovered, as long ago as that.

During the eighteenth century, wagon-ways were developed in many parts of northern Europe, and in a few places in America, and were used for moving stone, slate, coal and other heavy materials, from the mines or quarries where they were produced to the nearest navigable water. Few roads at that time were in a suitable state to be used even by pedestrians; to take heavy freight traffic on them was out of the question.

Normally, the trucks used on these old wagon-ways would be moved by gravity, the tracks being engineered to produce a sufficient fall. Where this was not possible, the trucks would be pulled by horses or mules, or pushed by labourers. The wooden rails were laid on oak sleepers and held in place with nails.

Then it was found that the wooden rails tended to wear and break down quickly where the track had a pronounced slope or curve, so lengths of iron plate were used as reinforcements where the rails most needed extra strength. The first rails made wholly of cast iron were produced at the Coalbrookdale Iron Works, in Shropshire, Great Britain. Abraham Darby, the proprietor of the works, had smelted more iron ore than he could sell, so he had it made into rails, intending to melt them down again when a customer appeared. The rails proved so satisfactory that he was persuaded to offer similar rails to mine owners in other parts of the country.

Above – A working model of Locomotion, the first passenger-hauling locomotive built in 1825 by Robert Stephenson.

Left – This model of George and Robert Stephensons' Rocket (built in 1829) shows it in its original form with the cylinders attached to the boiler in a steeply inclined position.

13 Left – *A museum quality ¾ in. scale model of the Talyllyn Railways narrow gauge 0–4–2 saddle tank locomotive. Talyllyn. The prototype was built in 1865.*

14 Left, below – *A 1¾ in. gauge model of the 'D', built by Frank Roberts of New Zealand. This locomotive and its companion works train were first made for Roberts' famous model railway.*

15 Above – *In the Smithsonian Institute, U.S. National Museum, Washington, D.C. there is this ½ in. scale model of the* Consolidation *(1866) - the first prototype 2-8-0 locomotive in the world.*

16 Below – *A model of a three-cylinder compound locomotive as introduced by F. W. Webb in 1881 on the London and North Western Railway.*

The first great step forward towards railways or railroads as we know them today was made by Richard Trevithick, a mine owner in Cornwall, Great Britain. Trevithick had certainly heard of the large steam-powered tricycle built by Nicholas Joseph Cugnot of Lorraine in 1769 that ran for twenty minutes at $2\frac{1}{4}$ miles per hour, and he knew, too, of the steam carriage produced by William Murdock in 1784. The Cornishman's great contribution to the history of transport was made when he saw how Cugnot's and Murdock's ideas could be applied to the primitive wagon-ways. His steam engines, mounted on wheels, can be safely regarded as the first railway locomotives.

Trevithick built his first steam carriage during 1800 and 1801. On Christmas Eve, 1801, he drove it part of the way up Beacon Hill, but it ran out of steam. Three days later, it was destroyed by fire. In 1803, he drove his second steam carriage in London, from Holborn to Paddington, but public opinion was not ready for the innovation, and it aroused no great interest. So, he returned to the construction of stationary engines, operating principally at Samuel Homfray's Ironworks at Pen-y-Darren, in South Wales.

Trevithick's next and most momentous locomotive was successfully tested on 21 February 1804, when it hauled five wagons, ten tons of iron and seventy men at a speed of nearly five miles per hour on the ten mile wagon-way between Merthyr Tydfil and Aber-

17 Constructed by P. Lottiaux in the scale 23 mm. to 1 metre, this is a model of a 0–4–6 compound locomotive of Paris, Lyons and Mediterranean railways, 1893; shown here on the Gur-Rug layout

cynon. The engine had a boiler 6 feet long, a return flue that brought the stack over the fire door, and four wheels, all power driven. Trevithick found that even with a smooth tread these wheels provided sufficient adhesion for use on iron rails of the type found on so many of the old wagon-ways. Unfortunately, the track at Abercynon, though made of cast iron rails on stone sleepers, did not prove strong enough to stand up to its unusual burden.

The possibilities opened up by Trevithick's new enterprise caused, this time, much excitement, and this was increased when, in 1808, he gave a series of demonstrations on a circular track near Euston Square, in London. There, behind a high fence, with an engine called *Catch-me-who-can* that could attain the frightening speed of twelve miles per hour, he showed to members of the public who had paid a small admission fee that steam was the great motive force of the future. The horse, as the prime means of fast travel, was on the way out.

The sensational success of Trevithick's demonstrations induced several other engineers to experiment in the same field. One of the first schemes to be operated profitably was suggested by John Blenkinsop, who managed a coal mine near Leeds, in the north of England. Blenkinsop invited Matthew Murray, who was a member of the local firm of Fenton, Murray and Woods, to design a loco-motive that would haul his trucks over the comparatively steep gradients between the mine and the town. The first Murray-Blenkinsop locomotive, running on rails that were fitted at one side (for safety on those up-and-down slopes) with a toothed rack, went into service in June 1812. In 1813, William Hedley, an engineer at Wylam Colliery, produced his famous *Puffing Billy*, and this was followed, in the next year, by George Stephenson's *Blucher*. All these were intended solely for the hauling of freight.

The lines that are generally assumed to have been the first used for the carriage of passengers were opened in 1803, between Wandsworth and Croydon, near London, and in 1804, the Oystermouth Railway. In these, horses were used for haulage. The first public railway to employ the new locomotive traction was suggested in 1818. This was intended to connect the two towns of Stockton and Darlington in the north of England. The railway was planned to have a single track, with passing places at intervals of a quarter of a mile. It was to be thirty-eight miles long.

George Stephenson, who had won an enviable reputation for himself by the success of the *Blucher* engine, was called in to supervise the construction of the new line. In 1822, when it was still in a far from finished state, he convinced the last waverers among the directors that they should use steam power on their railway, instead of animal traction. At the official opening, on 27 September 1825, Stephenson drove his own engine *Locomotion No. 1*. He had designed and built this especially for use on this historic occasion.

Even before the line was open, its fame had spread, and opinions were being expressed loudly for and against the new form of transport. The newspaper *John Bull* came out violently in opposition:

'The whole face of the kingdom is to be tattooed with these horrid things – huge mounds are to cut up our beautiful valleys; the noise and smell of locomotive steam-engines are to disturb the quiet of the farmer and gentleman . . .'

Other people prophesied that the smoke and fumes given off by the locomotives would be injurious to health and that cows frightened by them would cease to give milk, and hens to lay eggs. In spite of the shrill prognostications of those in the reactionary camp, many companies were formed to make railways to link more towns. On 24 May 1824, a meeting was held of those who were interested in the construction of a railway between Liverpool and Manchester. Up to that time the journey between the two towns had to be made by coach or carriage on deeply rutted roads which were quite unsuitable for the transportation of heavy loads, or by water, which was equally unsatisfactory – the canal between

19 Above A model in one-tenth natural size of Robert Stephenson der Adler, *built for the first German railway in 1835.*

20 Right – Another early German locomotive is the Bavaria. *The prototype was built by F. A. Maffei in 1844–45.*

21 *This model of the Netherlands Central Railways Class 41 2-2-[ ] was built in scale 1 to 10 by apprentices in the main repair she[ ] of Netherlands Railways in 1956-[ ] The prototype was built in 1899.*

the two busy places being frozen for much of the winter, and too low for barge traffic in the summer. The new railway line was planned to reduce the journey from thirty-six hours or more, to four or five.

When the line was nearly complete, the directors of the company that had been formed to construct it met to decide on the form of motive power that should be employed. On receiving a recommendation from their engineers that steam locomotives seemed to be the coming thing, they offered a generous money premium for the engine that would most nearly meet their requirements. It should be, they said, 'a decided improvement on any hitherto constructed'.

Five engines were entered for this famous competition. The locomotive judged by the public the most likely to win was the *Novelty*, constructed by J. Braithwaite and J. Ericsson, its position as popular favourite being due entirely to its elegant appearance. George Stephenson, working in conjunction with his son Robert, entered the rather less handsome *Rocket*. This locomotive had two cylinders, each 8 inches in diameter by 17 inches stroke, which were placed at the rear end of the boiler and inclined downward at an angle of 35° to the horizontal. The piston rods drove the front wheels, which were made of oak with iron tyres and had cast-iron bosses in which the crank pins were fitted. The three other engines

The North Brabant Dutch Railway Class 31 4–6–0 built in 1908 in Manchester were the first locomotives in the Netherlands with a bogie and three coupled axles. The model, scale 1 to 10, was built by C. J. Honig.

entered were the *Cyclopede*, the *Perseverance* and the *Sans Pareil*.

The trials were held on a level piece of the line one and three-quarters miles long, of which 220 yards at each end were allowed for starting and stopping. The competing engines were required to make ten double trips, going over the central section at full speed, which would represent a single journey from Manchester to Liverpool. Then, a fresh supply of water and fuel could be taken up before a second ten trips were attempted, to represent the return journey. To qualify, the locomotives had to travel at an average speed higher than ten miles per hour.

The first engine tested – the Stephensons' *Rocket* – was the most successful, attaining an average speed of 13.8 miles per hour. The *Novelty* had to be withdrawn from the competition when some of its boiler joints gave way; the *Sans Pareil* suffered from a broken feed pump; and the *Cyclopede* and *Perseverance* failed to sustain the required speed. The Stephensons, therefore, were awarded the prize, and the directors of the company declared themselves convinced, by the tests, of the suitability of the steam locomotive as a means of haulage.

The line was finished in the summer of 1830, and it was declared open on September 15th of that year by the Duke of Wellington, who was then Prime Minister of Great Britain. The opening ceremony caused great excitement:

'Liverpool was never so full of strangers, all the inns in the town were crowded to over-flowing and carriages stood in the streets all night, for want of room in stable yards.

On the morning of Wednesday, the people of the town and of the country began very early to gather near the railway. The weather was fine but dull. From before nine o'clock until ten the entrance of the station was crowded by splendid carriages from which people were alighting to seek their places as shown on their tickets. There were eight engines drawing thirty-three carriages filled with elegantly dressed persons. Each train had silken flags of different colours flying above the carriages. There were three bands playing, one of them in a carriage of one train.

The firing of a gun and the cheers of the crowd announced the arrival of the Duke of Wellington and his friends. The bands played "See the Conquering Hero Comes" and his railway carriage was attached to the Northumbrian locomotive engine . . . There were thousands of spectators who were kept out of the way by soldiers and railway police. A few minutes before eleven all was ready for the journey. The signal gun being fired, we started.'

During the six years that passed while the Liverpool and Manchester Railway was being planned and built, news of the new form of transport was being carried to other parts of the world.

In America, and on the continent of Europe, there were plenty of people ready to take an active interest. Wherever rails and horse-drawn or gravity-motivated wagons had been used for commercial freight purposes, people heard of the new steam-driven loco-motives and began to appreciate their advantages. One undertaking that was launched only a little too soon to be affected was the railroad opened on 7 October 1826 between Quincy and the Neponset River. This line was intended to carry granite for the Bunker Hill monument at Charlestown, Mass., and was the brain-child of Gridley Bryant.

The Baltimore and Ohio Railroad Company can claim to have the first railroad to be built in America for carrying, jointly, passengers and freight. The Company's charter was granted in 1827, and the first section of the line was opened to traffic in 1830 – it is exactly as old, that is, as the Liverpool and Manchester Railway. But, at first, horses were used for supplying the motive power, both for direct hauling and in treadmill engines, and it was some time before the directors of the company ventured to change over to steam. (In America, as in Britain, the new method of loco-motion aroused a certain amount of opposition. 'When it becomes necessary for man to travel beyond ten miles an hour,' thundered the editor of one Ohio newspaper, 'the Almighty will build him

Above, a working scale model of the locomotive Perseverance *built in England about 1855 for the Egyptian Government Railways.*

Below, model of an American Rio Grande Railway engine, built in 1870. It fetched more than £1,300 at a sale.

upon another pattern.') The original Baltimore and Ohio locomotive was built by Phineas Davis, who lost his life in 1835 in one
of the first derailments in railroad history.

The Delaware and Hudson Canal Company's railroad was
planned from the start with locomotive operation in view. In 1825,
the company, working in conjunction with the Pennsylvania
Association, despatched two engineers – William Strickland and
Horatio Allen – to England, to study the new system of transport.
The two men were charged to bring back all the relevant information they could possibly obtain:

'Locomotive machinery will command your attention and
inquiry. This is entirely unknown in the United States, and we
authorize you to procure a model of the most improved locomotive machine, at the expense of the society.'

The work was well done, and when Strickland travelled back to
Pennsylvania a year later he took with him an immense amount of
the most useful data and a persuasive model of an English locomotive. This can be seen, now, in the Franklin Institute at
Philadelphia. Allen, meanwhile, had contracted for the supply of
four different engines. The first of them, the locomotive *America*,
supplied by Robert Stephenson and Company, arrived in New
York on 15 January 1829. It was transported up the Hudson
River, and by canal from Rondout and is known to have reached
Eddyville on 16 July 1829. That, however, is the last record there
is of it, and it may never have been operated in America. The other
three locomotives ordered by Allen were the *Stourbridge Lion*, the
Delaware, and the *Hudson*, all built by Foster, Rastrick and
Company, of Stourbridge, Worcestershire, England. The *Lion*
reached New York on 13 May 1829. By August of that year it was
ready to make its trial trip, qualifying thereby for the honour of
being the first steam-powered locomotive ever to run on tracks in
the Western Hemisphere. When the trials had been completed,
the *Lion* was taken into service on the Delaware and Hudson
Company's lines.

Encouraged by the success of the Delaware and Hudson enterprise, a group of quick-thinking businessmen started to plan and
build the Charleston and Hamburg line. Their company, once it
had been properly constituted, was referred to as The South
Carolina Canal and Rail Road Company. This was the first
American railroad intended from the start for general public
passenger-carrying, and for locomotive operation. The first
scheduled service of any American railroad began on the lines
leading out of Charleston, South Carolina, on Christmas Day 1830.

After that, railroad companies were formed with varying degrees

ove, a model of a locomotive
igned by the American engineer
liam Norris in 1843. Austrian
ways acquired one, and the
del of this is depicted.

ow, John Stagg made this model
he Wildfire in 1839. The proto-
e was built for the Grand
ction Railway.

of vigour and efficiency in most parts of the American Continent. The Reading Company, which was originally incorporated in 1833 as the Philadelphia and Reading Railroad Company, and is thus one of the oldest railroad companies in the United States, claims (among other achievements) to have imported one of the first locomotives into the United States, to have bought the first of Matthias Baldwin's domestically produced full-sized locomotives – Baldwin had previously made a model, for demonstration purposes, for Peale's Philadelphia Museum – and to have pioneered the use, in America, of telegraphic communications for railroad working and the interlocking system of turnouts, or points, and signals. Today, with less than one-twelfth of the world's population, North America has close on a half of the world's railroad mileage and more than a half of the world's aggregate capacity for moving passengers and freight.

The first railway in France was opened in 1827. It ran from Saint-Etienne to Andrézieux, and like many early British and American lines it was intended mainly for the haulage of coal. At first – and indeed until 1844 – all the trucks were drawn by horses, and passengers were not carried until 1832.

On the Saint-Etienne–Lyons line, which was opened in 1830, steam locomotion was used from the beginning. In 1832, the French Government started to encourage, with great enthusiasm, the building of further lines. The main trunk routes from Paris to Nancy, Lille and other large towns were directly inspired by the central authority.

The year 1827 saw, too, the opening of the first section of railway in the Austrian Empire. The original concession for the line, which was to run from Budweis to Trojanov, had been granted in September 1824 to Franz Anton von Gerstner, who had built a short demonstration line in Vienna that virtually landed him the job. Having seen the railway well started, von Gerstner went off to Russia leaving its further construction in the capable hands of Mathias von Schönerer. The railway received royal approval in July 1832 when the Emperor Francis and the Empress Caroline Augusta rode in state from Magdalena to Anhof. A coach of this period is preserved to this day in the Technological Museum in Vienna. It looks exactly like a stage coach mounted carefully on railway wheels – which, in effect, is all that it was.

Ireland was the next country to experiment with railways – the first Irish line, from Dublin to Kingstown (Dun Laoghaire) was opened to traffic on 17 December 1834.

Then, in the following year, the first German railway was opened, running between Nuremberg and Fürth. The first steam locomotive to run successfully in Germany was *der Adler* (*The Eagle*), which was constructed in 1835.

Above – Models of early [co]aches built by Frank Roberts [a]re built to ½ in. scale, giving a [tra]ck gauge of 1¾ in.

Centre – Also modelled by [Fr]ank Roberts are two early loco-[mo]tives from the U.S., a Class 'K' [le]ft) and a Class 'Q' (centre), and [on] the right a Class 'L' built in [Ne]w Zealand in 1903.

Below – A further selection of [loc]omotives and old type rolling [sto]ck made by Frank Roberts and [sho]wn at the Romance of Transport [Ex]hibition.

There had been at least two unsuccessful attempts to introduce steam locomotion into Germany before this. In 1815, Herr Krigar, the Superintendent of the Royal Iron Foundry, had visited Britain with a Herr Eckardt. There, they are believed to have studied the Murray-Blenkinsop rack engines made shortly before. Within three years, two engines that were very like the Murray-Blenkinsop prototypes had been constructed at the German foundry. One was put into service at Gliewitz in 1816, but it was not a success. The second, intended for service at Saarbrucken, was designed to draw coal from the pits to the River Saar, but that, too, was a failure. It was sold for old iron in 1835, the same year *der Adler* was built.

In Germany, as had happened in France, a systematic plan of trunk lines was intended, but the division of the country into a number of independent states made this aim difficult to realise. It turned out most fortunately in the end that the lines in the various states had been made to a uniform gauge or width. This unity resulted from the wholesale importation of British locomotives and rolling stock, and it saved much expense and inconvenience when the systems were amalgamated, after 1847.

The first railway to be constructed in Russia – a short line in the vicinity of St Petersburg (now Leningrad) – was completed in 1847. By the end of the nineteenth century there were 31,675 miles miles of railway track in the whole of the Russian Empire.

European countries that caught the railway fever in the years between 1837 and 1850 included Denmark, Switzerland, Sweden and Spain. Italy – divided, like Germany, into a number of separate states – was not yet ready for a national system of railways. After the Act of Union in 1861, steps were immediately taken to provide the whole country with a network of lines.

The first Australian line was opened as a result of private enterprise in 1854 near Melbourne, Victoria. This was followed, in the next year, by the standard gauge system of New South Wales, and lines were soon developed to serve parts of South Australia, Queensland, and Western Australia. In Argentina, the first six miles of track were laid in 1857. By 1969, the total in that country had increased to over 27,000 miles!

26 *J. A. Maffei built this type 78 4–6–0 locomotive in Munich for the Netherlands Central Railway in 1910–11. It was nicknamed the 'Zeppelin' because of the shape of the smokebox door. The model, to a scale of 1 to 13, was made by H. A. Driesen in 1917–20.*

Railways came comparatively late to Japan. The first line was not opened in that country until 1872. During the next twenty years, privately owned systems were developed side by side with the state lines, but in spite of this joint effort by 1887 only 240 miles of track had been laid. Today, the state-owned Japanese lines cover nearly 9,000 miles, are served by some of the fastest expresses in the world (they manage to move people around at speeds greater than 130 miles per hour without causing them any marked discomfort or inconvenience) and are second in importance, in Asia, only to the railways of India.

Before the end of the nineteenth century, it had been made possible for people to travel across whole continents without having to disembark and change trains. An Imperial Commission was set up in 1857 to inquire into 'the advisability of constructing a trans-continental line of railway through British territory from the Atlantic to the Pacific Ocean.' One of the Commission's first actions was to appoint a Captain Palliser to lead a surveying party. After four years' work, Palliser reported that there was little, if any, chance of such a railroad being constructed. But Palliser was wrong. Twenty-five years later, in 1886, the first Canadian Pacific trans-continental train travelled from Montreal to Port Moody (now called Vancouver), a distance of nearly 3,000 miles, in six days.

After that, lines that could carry passengers and freight at high speeds across enormous distances started to proliferate, one of the most famous – to this day – being the Trans-Siberian Railway. This was built between 1894 and 1904 and has an over-all length, from Stalingrad to Vladivostock, of 5,973 miles.

Wherever railways spread, over the surface of the globe, they were quickly followed by the models that are the subject of this book. In at least one instance it is certainly true to say that the models were there first. When a new railway was to be built in Nigeria in 1911, models made to a scale of $\frac{3}{4}$ inch to 1 foot were commissioned and presented to the Emir of Zara and the Emir of Katsina. They had never seen a railway, and the models showed them what the locomotives that were about to run on their lands would really look like.

*A fine 3½ in. gauge model of a
-4–0 American wood-burning
comotive with its tender built by
. S. Holt. This model was
varded the New Zealand Cup at
e 1968 Model Engineer
xhibition.*

3 The Origins of Railway Modelling

Nobody knows exactly how, or when, or where people began to make models of railways. No one can say positively of any small replica of an early locomotive, 'There you see the first model engine that ever was made'. No one can claim, beyond any shadow of doubt, to own the one authentic miniature that started thousands of dedicated craftsmen, all over the world, on their quest for perfection. All we can say for certain is that the earliest railway models were made for practical, rather than aesthetic, purposes. The man who first felt the magic of railways, and tried to reproduce the objects of his admiration on a smaller scale came a little later.

There is a strong possibility that Matthew Murray, who built the geared-for-safety rack engines for John Blenkinsop's coal mine near Leeds, in England, was actually the first man ever to make a model locomotive. Certainly, it is known that in 1812 he made two replicas of the engine that was already running successfully – each replica being one-twelfth the size of the original. Murray gave one of the models to his sponsor, John Blenkinsop, who used it for showing other mine managers the advantages of steam locomotion. The other, Murray packed off to the Czar of Russia, hoping to interest that powerful man in the value of railways. The model Murray gave to Blenkinsop was passed on, eventually, to a man named Embleton who was the next manager of the mine. It remained in the possession of the family for many years until, on the death of Embleton's son, it was put up for sale by auction and purchased for a collection in the United States.

The Czar's present and the model locomotive taken to America in 1826 by William Strickland at the instance of the Delaware and Hudson Canal Company were not the only railway replicas to leave England even before the Liverpool and Manchester Railway was open. In 1829, Johann Wolfgang von Goethe, the great German poet and man of letters, was sent a miniature version of the Stephensons' award-winning locomotive *Rocket*, together with a set of wagons and rails. As an elderly and very grand intellectual might have been expected to do, he passed these on to his grandsons Walter and Wolfgang. By his benevolent action he may well have made them the first of a'l the millions of young

Above – A painted wooden toy engine made about 1880. The train consists of two coaches, two freight cars and a luggage van.

Centre – Made by R. Ockleford 1850, this 5 in. gauge brass model is of the Stockton and Darlington Railway 2–2–2 locomotive agnet *built in 1832.*

Below – A toy locomotive of ? *type used in the 1860's, made* ?brass and marked 'Stephenson', ?wered by steam with a two-?inder engine. 65 mm. gauge.*

43

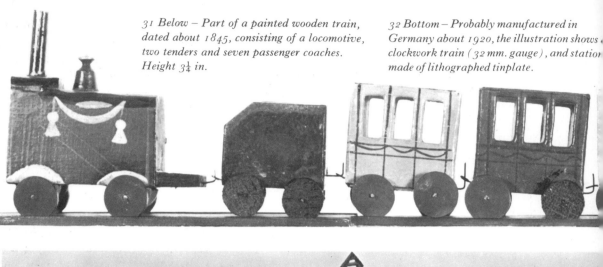

31 Below – Part of a painted wooden train, dated about 1845, consisting of a locomotive, two tenders and seven passenger coaches. Height 3¼ in.

32 Bottom – Probably manufactured in Germany about 1920, the illustration shows clockwork train (32 mm. gauge), and station made of lithographed tinplate.

people who have received gifts of model railways, and who have been made ecstatically happy by their good fortune.

Nobody knows who first set out to make railway models with the conscious intention of selling those models for profit.

We do know, though, that during the 1830s and 1840s astute manufacturers in several different parts of the world were producing crude and inexpensively made toys that distantly resembled trains. Birmingham, England, became an important centre for the production of cheap tinplate models. Wooden locomotives and freight cars intended for the nurseries of very young children were exported in large numbers from Germany and other northern European countries. By 1850 there were several American firms busily engaged in the production of trackless locomotives and cars that were designed to be pulled across playroom floors on lengths of string. Among the earliest manufacturers of these toys were the Merriam Manufacturing Company, of Durham, Connecticut; Hull and Stafford, of Clinton, Connecticut; and Francis, Field and Francis, of Philadelphia. A little later came James Fallows and Company, of Philadelphia, which brand marked its toys IXL (I Excel). Collectors now pay large sums for genuine examples of these comparatively crude models, seeing them as direct links with the pioneers who thrust forward, in spite of all hazards and dangers, into the wild West, and built railroads to every part of the continent.

Nobody knows who made the first railway model that was entirely self-propelled.

We do know, though, that in the 1830s an energetic Kentucky showman, Joseph Bruen, had a model locomotive with a short length of portable track, and that he took his small railroad on tour, carrying the component parts in a wagon. When he reached a suitable centre of population, he would set out the railroad – aided, usually, by someone he had hired on the spot – and then he would invite people to take rides, for a small charge. He is said to have made substantial sums of money by this enterprise.

We know, too, that in the summer of 1838 the members of the Mechanics' Institution at Leeds, Great Britain, set up an exhibition to which scholars, students and apprentices were admitted by season ticket. One of the exhibits attracted an unusual amount of attention. In the centre of a miniature lake, the men who had organized the exhibition had made, with rocks and ferns, a miniature island. Around the outer edge of the island they arranged a miniature railway line, and on this line ran, with a bravura that was entirely appropriate to an occasion that may have been historic, a small model locomotive. Concealed in the rocks and ferns, the mechanic who had been appointed to operate the little engine had to work with furious abandon just to make it go. With a pair of

household bellows he puffed energetically at the glowing charcoal in the tiny firebox in a frantic attempt to raise sufficient steam. At first, the engine sulked, and refused to do anything more exciting than letting out an occasional spurt of hot, oily water in the faces of the eager spectators.

Then, to the sound of loud cheers, it started to move, and make a slow, majestic circuit of the island. After the man in charge had done some more puffing, it set off again – this time, having hot, dry cylinders, at a greater speed. Around and around the island it went, at an ever-increasing pace, until at last, unable to sustain the burden of its sudden blaze of glory, it screamed off the lines

33 Top – The Aquarius *was one of the broad-gauge locomotives of the Netherlands Rhine Railway. The model was made in Amsterdam by J. T. F. Steenbergen in 1846 to scale of 1 to 7.5.*

34 Below – A coal-fired model, built to one-quarter scale on 5 in gauge, of No. 684 0–4–0 WT Jack*. The prototype was used for hauling clay.*

and plunged with a dramatic hiss into the lake. The salvage of the little locomotive after this miniature tragedy drew even larger crowds than its maiden run.

It is safe to say that scale models, produced individually by fine craftsmen purely for their creators' pleasure, began to appear in reasonably large numbers in almost every country almost as soon as railways were an established feature of the landscape. Fine specimens dating from the late 1830s and the 1840s can be found in many different parts of the world. To take a fairly typical example – there is, in the Museum of British Transport at Clapham, London, a scale model of the locomotive *Wildfire* made by a clever craftsman named John Stagg of Birmingham, in 1839. The prototype was built by Robert Stephenson and Company only two years before, being Number 8 in the company's stock. It was used to draw the first train on the opening day of the Grand Junction Railway – a distinction which may have inspired John Stagg to reproduce it in miniature.

Not many of the very earliest railway models are represented in contemporary pictures, but there are, again, a few notable examples. In the Science Museum, in London, there is a fine model locomotive made principally of copper and brass that has irrefutable associations with the origins of the famed Great Western Railway. Most of the early locomotives of that historically important line had large driving wheels with small boilers and cylinders. As a result of that unfortunate combination, they were not really powerful enough, and gave a considerable amount of trouble. The best of the stable was probably Stephenson's *North Star*. Daniel Gooch, appointed to assist Isambard Kingdom Brunel in the locomotive department, designed a standard broad gauge engine that was based largely on the *North Star*, and this proved very successful. The model of this early paragon that stands now in the Science Museum must have been one of the most treasured possessions of Daniel Gooch, for it is shown prominently in a photograph of the great designer taken in 1845, when he was no more than twenty-nine years old.

That, then, is just about all we know for certain about how, and when, and where, the making of model trains actually started. But everyone who has any interest at all in the subject is constantly on the lookout for old models that will add even a small fraction to the sum-total of knowledge. Examples as venerable as those described in this chapter may turn up unrecognized, at any time, in undisturbed homes, or in junk shops, or at jumble sales. They may be recovered, unexpectedly, from attics and cellars. In these acquisitive days they are not likely to remain unacclaimed for long. The shophounds are out, looking for primitive railway models, and they have exceptionally keen noses, and apparently bottomless pockets.

4 The Commercial World

People who are interested in model railways can be divided, roughly, into two categories – those who are content to buy the models, and those who, wishing to use their own skills, or unable to find ready-made models of the prototypes they admire most, are prepared to make them. As there are more people in the ready-to-go-shopping category, if the reckoning is made on a global basis, the commercial world must be considered first.

The man who first thought of producing model trains for sale in large quantities started one of the world's most thriving industries. He was a considerable benefactor, too. At the present time, the great manufacturers such as Märklin, Rovex, Fleischmann, Rivarossi, Arnold, Athearn and LIMA are probably providing as many hours of pleasure for as many different people as any other comparable number of commercial enterprises of any other kind, anywhere.

The history of the development of any large company is always liable to be eventful and exciting, but no tale of success was ever based more surely on solid achievement than that of the House of Märklin. In 1914, Märklins employed only 600 people. Today, more than 2,000 workers are busy in the main factory at Göppingen, in Württemberg, and two more factories have had to be opened in the Rems Valley to keep up with the many and varied requirements of Märklin enthusiasts.

The business was started by Theodor Märklin who was the son of a parson. He settled in the little town of Göppingen in 1840, gaining full civic rights in 1856 and becoming an independent master tinsmith at the same time. In 1859 he married Karoline Hettich of Ludwigsburg, and it seems both fitting and romantic that it was his new wife who suggested in addition to his other lines he should make some miniature pots and pans that could be sold as Christmas presents for children. Probably, she had seen and had been delighted by the toy kitchens that had been made in the previous century at Nuremberg. Herr Märklin's new nursery-size kitchenware sold rapidly. The good Karoline had started something big. She played an energetic part in building up the business, too, and developed what can truly be called a sales organization. It

Taken in 1886 outside the [pre]mises of Mr Bassett-Lowke's [gra]ndparents, the photograph [sho]ws, from left to right : Mr and [Mr]s Bassett (the grandparents), [W]. J. Bassett-Lowke, his [mot]her, father and uncle.

would probably be fair to call her the first female commercial traveller, as she journeyed throughout Southern Germany and Switzerland to promote the sales of the toys. Soon, her husband had to acquire larger factory premises.

But fate stepped in. In 1866, Theodor Märklin died through the effects of an accident. His widow struggled to keep the business going for the sake of her three sons, but without her husband's knowledge and enterprise, she could not prevent the decline of the firm, and before long there was no money to pay the employees' wages.

In 1888, Theodor's three sons Eugen, Wilhelm, and Karl started the business again, virtually without capital. Wilhelm was a skilled tinsmith who had been working in the United States; Eugen and Karl were expert metal pressers. At first the young men were too poor to employ any assistants, and they had to obtain their materials on credit.

But they were also industrious and clever. Before many months had passed, their firm – known, ever since, as Märklin Brothers – had produced commercially the first tinplate model railways with switches, or points, and crossings. Almost certainly, Wilhelm would have seen while he was in America some of the crude, string-pulled floor runners that were by that time so popular as toys, and these had inspired him to go one better. Wherever they were exhibited, the Märklins' little track layouts – each of which would normally be made in the shape of a figure 8, with or without additions – drew admiring crowds. When one of these layouts was shown at the Leipzig Spring Fair of 1891 it caused such a stir that the Märklin brothers decided to throw in their lot with the wealthy E. F. von Plochingen. Suitably financed by him, they were able to embark on ambitious schemes of mass-production, and by 1900 they had acquired a factory in the Stuttgarter Strasse at Göppingen that covered some 65,000 square feet. In their first year at this factory they were able to produce in enormous quantities toy trains worked by live steam, as well as the first electrically operated railway models to be made commercially in Europe.

Not surprisingly, the enviable successes of the Märklin brothers encouraged other European manufacturers to see themselves as potential competitors. Among the earliest were the Bing brothers, who actually became, for a short time, the largest toymakers in the world.

The Bing brothers had been producing toys in Nuremberg since 1865. Following the Märklins' example, they set out to help satisfy the new public appetite for reasonably cheap railway models that would work more satisfactorily than the hissing, leaking 'dribblers' that had been marketed by a few manufacturers during the previous decade. With enormous energy, the brothers set out to

These four photographs from early Märklin catalogues show:

36 Above – A selection of rolling stock;

37 Above right – a train set for pulling with string;

38 Centre right – a model of der Adler (compare with the model p. 31);

39 Right – Rocket

Selbstausweichende Karrenzüge ohne Mechanik ohne Schienen.

Karren-Züge, 3 rädrige Lokomotiven und Wagen ohne Schienen.
Stabile Bauart in Blech und Eisen, sorgfältig lackiert, bequem zu verkuppeln. Spurweite 8,5 cm.

Erstklassige Neuheit, mit der, durch einfaches geometrisches Gesetz, Wagenzüge von beliebiger Länge, lediglich durch die Direktion von vorne, genau in gewünschter Richtung gehalten werden.

Selbst vordere konträre Fahrt wird von den hinteren Wagen getreulich eingehalten.

Auch das kleine Kind vermag die Züge zwischen Hindernissen jeglicher Art hindurchzulavieren.

No. 8490 L.	Lokomotive ohne Uhrwerk	18,5 cm lang.
„ 8490/1.	Kippwagen, grau	18,5 „ „
„ „ /2.	Kohlenwagen, grün	18,5 „ „
„ „ /3.	Geländerwagen, weiss	18,5 „ „
„ „ /4.	Viehwagen, gelb	18,5 „ „
„ „ /5.	Holzwagen, mit Kette, grün	18,5 „ „
„ „ /6.	Kastenwagen, blau	18,5 „ „

No. 8490 L.   p. St.   No. 8490 G/4.   p. St.   No. 8490 G/6.   p. St.

No. 8490/1   2   3   4   5   6   „ 8490 GL/4.   „ 8490 GL/6.

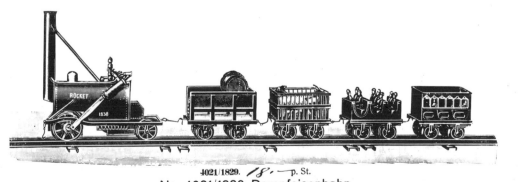

4021/1829. *18·* — p. St.

No. 4021/1829 Dampfeisenbahn.

Modell des historischen Zugs mit Lokomotive „Rocket" aus dem Jahr 1829. Ergötzlicher Kontrast gegenüber den verfeinerten Zügen der Gegenwart. Die Garnitur besteht aus: Lokomotive, Kohlenwagen mit Fässchen, Viehwagen mit Vieh, 2 offene Personenwagen mit Figuren, 8 runde Schienen 1601A, 4D.

Zuglänge . . . . 83 cm

capture as many as they could of the expanding world markets, manufacturing more than 250 different cars at the same time, with complete lines intended for the United States, Canada, Great Britain, and the various countries of Europe. It has been estimated that over the years Bing exported more than seventy-five different types of American car, all correctly lettered with a suitable road name. Today, early examples of Bing railway models, unrestored and in reasonably good condition, fetch as large sums in the open American market as many legitimate works of art.

There were other manufacturers, besides Märklin and Bing, whose early models are keenly sought by collectors. There was Georges Carette, for instance – a shrewd Frenchman who set up his factory in Nuremberg, attracted there by the relatively low wages asked for by the German craftsmen, and by their fantastic skill. Karl Bub made less finely finished and less expensive trains, and their models, in consequence, do not fetch as high prices in public salerooms. But Karl Bub took over some of the Bing dies when Bing finally went out of business, and in that way the company earned a secure place in the pages of model-railway history.

On the other side of the Atlantic Ocean, the model railroad scene was dominated for nearly a quarter of a century by the great firm of Ives. Known throughout the United States during the 1880s and 1890s for their trackless toy trains, Ives first introduced clockwork track models into their lists in 1901. From that year until the company ran into financial difficulties at the time of the Great Depression, Ives made and sold railroad models of exemplary quality and value. They undertook to repair or replace them if necessary, too, on terms that were astonishingly generous. The firm's ultimate insolvency is believed to have been due, in part, to this philanthropic policy.

In most fields of human activity there are certain figures that make the majority of their contemporaries seem like pygmies. In the world of model railways, one of the most influential personalities was Wenman J. Bassett-Lowke, who first started to make an impact on the trade at the end of the nineteenth century. Young Bassett-Lowke had been apprenticed at his father's general engineering works in Northampton, England. A keen model-maker in his spare time, he felt frustrated by the difficulty of obtaining well-designed and accurately produced components. So he decided to make and sell these himself.

Quickly, young Bassett-Lowke's enterprise started to thrive. He had charm, and the most potent personal magnetism, as well as considerable business acumen. He was able to make use of all the facilities of his father's factory. His friends on the staff were ready to help him. A useful ally was the firm's book-keeper, Harry F. R.

A clockwork engine made by Hornby in Gauge OO of an 0–4– tank in London North Eastern Railway livery, in the collection o Master Russell Beckwith.

Franklin, who counted the coins as they poured into the till. The first Bassett-Lowke Catalogue was advertised in 1899 in the paper called *The Model Engineer*. Almost before its contents had had a chance to be properly digested, the young man's mail order business was bringing in more commissions than he could easily fulfil.

In 1900, Wenman Bassett-Lowke made a journey that altered the whole history of model railways – he visited the Paris Exhibition. There he saw some miniature steam engines shown by the principal German manufacturers. These engines had novel, double-acting cylinders, and they were made to precision limits that Bassett-Lowke had never encountered before – never, that is, in the toy or miniature engineering field. He returned to England entirely dissatisfied with the crude locomotives, cobbled up to no specified scale or proportion, that had been made and sold there in the previous ten years. In a changed, highly critical frame of mind he started to create new, true-to-scale designs, causing a small sensation with the $1\frac{3}{4}$ inch gauge express locomotive *Lady of the Lake* that he marketed in great quantities in 1901.

At that stage, another bright star had already started to move in the model engineering firmament. His name was Henry Greenly, and he came from a family that had been involved in the transport business for several generations, Greenlys having been makers of stage coaches during the eighteenth century and officials on the railways that replaced them. Henry Greenly was a brilliant craftsman and Bassett-Lowke was quick to recognize his talents. Employed as a consulting engineer, Greenly defined a series of standard gauges, each of which could be related, in true scale, to the prototype. It is typical of Greenly's competence that these gauges are the basis of those still used by model railway makers today.

During the next three decades, Bassett-Lowke and Greenly worked in the closest harmony. Both believed passionately in the importance of working to scale. All the engines with which they were associated, in their complementary capacities as designer and manufacturer, had to look like real engines reduced to miniature proportions. In the commercial field, the aim was a new one.

Besides working with each other in the greatest sympathy, Bassett-Lowke and Greenly also established excellent working relationships with Bing and the other leading Nuremberg firms. It would be difficult to say which – the German firms or the British – owed most to the other, since the Germans were constantly reminded by Bassett-Lowke and Greenly of the importance of working exactly to a prototype, while the British men were able to study, in return, the Germans' superb metal-working techniques and ingenious mass-production methods.

...dern Gauge HO equipment ...e by a commercial firm.

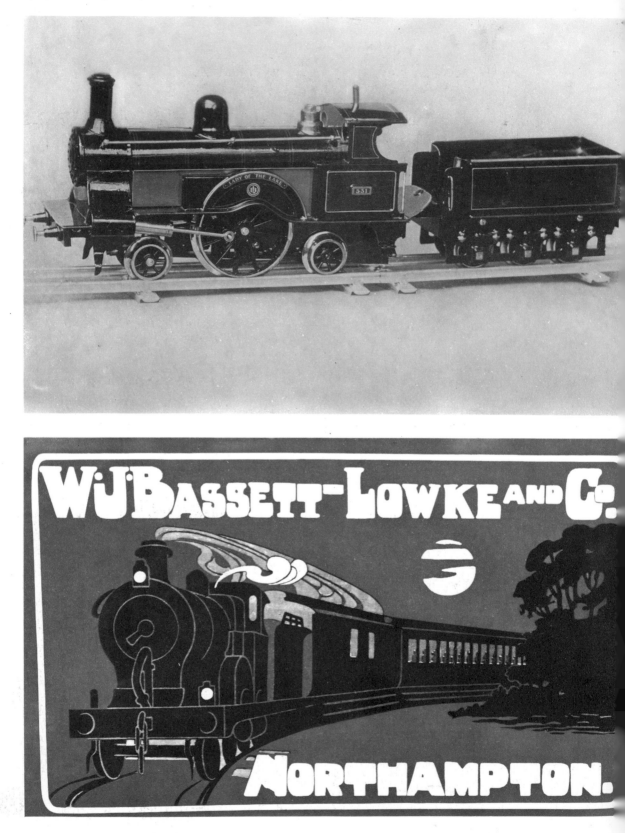

42 Above – An early version of the London and North Western Railway Black Prince. *A low pressure steam model in 2½ in. gauge.*

Left – The first quantity produced Bassett-Lowke steam locomotive, the Lady of the Lake, *made in 1901.*

Below, left – An early Bassett-Lowke catalogue cover.

43 Below – This Gauge OO electric model railway was made in 1922. It demonstrated the practical possibility of miniature gauge model railways.

In 1908, Bassett-Lowke decided to open a London showroom, and the firm's new premises in High Holborn quickly became a magnetic attraction for visitors to the British capital. Among the wealthy customers drawn to this, the most famous at that time of all model railway showrooms, was the Maharajah of Jodhpur, who ordered a mammoth and magnificent train set for the grounds of his favourite palace. Shortly after, Bassett-Lowkes' was visited by the Maharajah's rival, the Maharajah of Udaipur. Told by the shrewd showroom manager of the former's purchases, the Maharajah promptly ordered for his own estates a set of the same kind, only twice as large and three times as splendid.

Walt Disney, creator of Mickey Mouse and maestro of Disneyland, used to make the Bassett-Lowke showroom his first port of call whenever he visited England.

As Bassett-Lowke's fame spread to all parts of the world, so, too, did that of the House of Märklin, the directors of which have always managed to keep a little ahead of developments in the world of real railways. The Cologne-to-Bonn Rhine Bank Electric Railway had hardly been opened in 1905, amid universal acclaim, before Märklins brought out their miniature version of the sensational prototype. The Märklin model train, driven, like the original, by electricity, was made for Gauge 1 only, and measured just over 51 inches long.

44 An industrial diesel locomotive in Gauge 1 with plastic body and diecast metal frame made by Märklin.

*Also made by Märklin in Gauge 1
this is a model of the German
Federal Railways Class 80 tank
locomotive, with exact reproduction of the Heusinger drive
rod system.*

Märklins, too, have been instrumental in introducing many new model-making techniques. For a time, the firm deliberately reduced, in one respect, the range of its commitments, giving up the production of Gauge 2 models in 1918, Gauge 1 models in 1935, and Gauge 0 models in 1955. By taking these steps, Märklins placed themselves in a position to devote the whole of their energies to the further technical development of the up-to-date Gauge HO. This allowed the firm to reach, within their deliberately chosen limits, the highest possible degree of perfection, and now every Märklin innovation is awaited, all over the world, with intense interest. Recently, the company has started the production of Gauge 1 models again, for the first time since before the Second World War.

In the explosive expansion of commercial and industrial activity that followed the end of those hostilities, several model railway manufacturing companies managed to build themselves up rapidly to reach levels of resourcefulness and competence that had been achieved in the previous decades only by such great houses as Märklin, Bing and Ives. One of the most extraordinary post-war success stories concerns the lively Italian company called LIMA which now exports models of great excellence to more than fifty countries.

The name LIMA is formed from the initial letters of the full name: LAVORAZIONE ITALIA METALLI ED AFFINI which the company translates roughly as: Italian Working of Metals and Affinities. Founded in 1949, for the first nine years of its existence LIMA produced miniature automobiles, motor boats and toys of other kinds, but no model trains.

Then, after an intensive study of the market, the directors of the company decided to have some train models constructed in HO Gauge. These were put on the market at competitive prices and immediately proved popular. So, the directors decided to enter the model railway field in a bigger way. They caused many other models of different trains to be constructed, and gradually curtailed the production of their other lines. Now LIMA produces only electric trains. The manufacture of all other models and toys has been abandoned by the company.

The upsurge of interest in model railways after the Second World War brought a new lease of life, too, to certain older companies, such as Fleischmann, whose products are now universally admired.

In the year 1887, an engraver and modeller called Jean Fleischmann started a business at Number 3, Martin-Behaim Strasse, Nuremberg. After a few years, he began to manufacture magnetic toy animals and model ships. The enterprise prospered, and in 1899 Fleischmann set up a department to produce exact models of

46 Made by Lima in Italy this Gauge N model is a type GP30 diesel in Union Pacific livery. Its length is slightly over four inches.

real ocean-going liners. Many of these can be seen today in the principal museums of the world.

In 1940, Herr Fleischmann's widow made the business over to her sons, Johan and Emil. Even at that time, it was potentially of interest to model railway enthusiasts, because two years earlier Fleischmanns' had bought up and digested the firm of Doll and Company who specialized in making steam engines. But before the Second World War had ended, much of Fleischmanns' manufacturing plant had been destroyed, and when peace came the enterprise had to be started again, virtually from scratch.

In 1949, the year of the birth of LIMA, Fleischmanns began the production of electrically driven Gauge O model railways, using the most up-to-date systems of current supply. In 1952 their programme was extended to include Gauge HO models, and these have proved the most generally popular. Today, the firm, with manufacturing plants in Nuremberg, Heilsbronn and Dinkelsbühl, is numbered among the largest international toy manufacturers. The Fleischmann magazines *Fleischmann Kurier* (published in German, four times a year) and *Fleischmann Revue* (published in French and Dutch, annually) contain much interesting and informative material about railways, both real and miniature.

The development of sophisticated plastic-moulding techniques during the war years brought revolutionary changes in the pro-

7 A type CC 68000 diesel locomotive of the French National Railways made in Gauge HO by Fleischmann.

48 This is a model of a class 50
2–10–0 multi-purpose locomotive
of German Federal Railways made
by Fleischmann in Gauge HO.

49 An unusual wheel arrangement,
4–8–8–2, is shown on this model
of the Southern Pacific Lines
'Hudson' locomotive modelled by
Rivarossi in Gauge HO. Notice
the cab in a forward position.

cesses by which railway models are manufactured. One of the leaders in this field has been the enterprising Italian firm of Rivarossi, which began its activity in 1945 in a village near Como, using a two-car garage newly equipped for the production of model trains. Rivarossi now employs more than 300 people (many more, if one includes those employed by sub-contractors) who produce models of the highest possible standard.

Equally energetic has been the British firm of Rovex Industries, who, as Rovex Plastics Limited, set out in 1949, to produce realistic and reliable plastic train sets at reasonable prices. For months, the Rovex people struggled with production difficulties. Then, after a frantic 48-hour non-stop rush, they delivered their first train sets to a multiple store in Kingston in Surrey. Within a few hours, every one of these had been sold, and the success of the enterprise was certain. Now, Rovex models (known, usually, by the trade name Triang-Hornby) are produced in Australia, France, New Zealand and South Africa, as well as at the parent factory at Margate, in Great Britain.

The aim of the Rovex management is essentially a practical one. They know that their models are not likely to be used only by adults – small boys like to play with model trains, too, and there is nothing more frustrating to the young than to see a handsome train set and to be told. 'You must not touch it.' So, the Rovex design staff are urged to make the company's model trains as robust and as easy to service as possible. Big selling features on Triang-Hornby models are the small magnets they build into many of the understructures to make the models adhere more safely to the track. This has the same effect as increasing the weight of the models, without adding visibly to their bulk.

The mass production of one single railway model by modern methods is a large-scale industrial enterprise. It cannot be undertaken unless a manufacturer is prepared to invest a considerable amount of money in the preparation of the necessary moulds. These can only be used in conjunction with extremely expensive machines, and, they require many weeks, possibly months, of highly skilled work to prepare. So, steps have to be taken to make sure that the time and the money that are spent on a new line are going to yield a satisfactory return.

The manufacturer's first big worry concerns his choice of prototype. Making this decision alone is time-consuming. He must find out – often, by elaborate schemes of market research – what the customers in countless model shops are going to want, a season or two ahead. He may be guided, in making his decision, by suggestions he has received from retailers, or would-be customers, or by opinions expressed in the model railway press. His verdict, in the last analysis, may be largely a subjective one, for he will

50 *The G.W.R. 4–2–2* Lord of the Isles, *a model made by Rovex. The 7 feet 8 inch driving wheels on the prototype are worthy of note. The model was discontinued in 1964.*

51 *The Rivarossi model of a two-unit Northern Pacific diesel in Gauge HO.*

52 *A model of the type 141–R locomotive of the French National Railways manufactured by Gerard–Tab in Gauge HO.*

53 *In Gauge N, this is a model of the type 231 (Pacific) Grand Trunk Western livery made by Atlas.*

undoubtedly be a railway enthusiast, with his own pronounced likes and dislikes. Nevertheless, a decision will only be made after lengthy consultations with all the heads of the departments concerned – Management, Development, Sales, Buying, Production, Servicing, Publicity and Pricing will all want a say in the matter.

Having settled on a design that will be novel enough to make a real impact on the market (the Sales Director will frown on any proposed line that in his view is too like any other model already on sale) the manufacturer, or someone acting for him, has next to obtain the fullest possible information about the prototype. Most railway companies are pleased to supply the great commercial concerns with the necessary working drawings, but these, which consist usually of side elevations and end views, have to be supplemented whenever practicable with specially taken photographs. Views taken of the top of the prototype from directly above are particularly important, since a great many young people still hurry to lay down their first model-railway tracks on the family's living-room floor, and this is the angle from which these customers will view their models!

Before, even, the project has gone this far, technical experts will have been considering how the model may be produced in the most economical way. Sometimes, savings may be made by standardization. An important and expensive item – the chassis

54 A Trix model in Gauge HO of one of the electric locomotives used by the German Federal Railway. The Pantograph is shown in the raised position.

5 Also in Gauge HO, this model represents a typical electric locomotive used by the Japanese National Railways.

of a locomotive, say, or the underframe of a coach – may be so nearly like that produced for some other model that the same part can be used for both without lowering the required standards of exactness. (Occasionally, an especially keen-eyed amateur will spot some slight divergence between a model and its prototype that has been caused by the manufacturer's decision to use an interchangeable part. This invariably produces a scandalized letter of protest in the model railway press and is not good for trade.)

So, the production picture will have been roughly planned, even before the Development Department takes over, but the detailed drawings that are made next, over a period of weeks, by the most sensitive and skilled draughtsmen that the manufacturer can persuade to enter his service will establish to within limits of five-thousandths of an inch the final shape of the model that eventually will be sent off, carefully packed, in thousands to retailers all over the world.

As soon as these fabulously exact drawings have been completed, and checked, and checked yet again, a proving model will be made by skilled craftsmen in a small workshop. These craftsmen will work to the measurements shown on the drawings, using knives, files and other hand tools, and they will use as far as possible the materials of which the mass-produced models are to be made. If the draughtsman has made a single mistake, which is unlikely, and if the checkers have missed it, which is even more unlikely, this is the stage at which it will be discovered. It is the stage, too, at which many production problems will be solved before they have even arisen. Undercuts, insufficient allowances for withdrawal (draw angles) and other factors in a design that may interfere seriously with the moulding processes are much more easily seen when a three-dimensional model is inspected than they are when the model is just a drawing on paper.

All being well, the drawings go next to the mould-makers. These are men who have acquired their impressive skills only after years of the most arduous training. They may take months to finish the steel moulds that will, eventually, form the mass-produced models. To reproduce the intricate mechanical details that are barely visible in the proving model even with the aid of a magnifying glass, the mould-makers will probably make, in wood, a model of their own that is three or four times the required size. They then use a reducing machine called a pantograph, for cutting in reverse or negative form these almost microscopic shapes in the moulds.

Few of the young people who buy, or are given, a beautiful new plastic-bodied locomotive, coach or other commercially produced railway model will realize how few seconds have to elapse – once the precious moulds have been made – before its gleaming, highly detailed shape has been finally achieved. The raw material is made up in small pellets, like bird food. This is poured into a hopper at the top of an injection-moulding machine. From this hopper, the material drops by the good old-fashioned force of gravity into a cylinder in which it is heated and compressed, so that it forms a soft, homogeneous mass. When it is completely softened, it is forced into the mould at a pressure of at least six tons. It takes only a few seconds for the softened plastic to fill all the tiniest recesses in the mould and to chill. When it has hardened, it is ejected as a perfectly formed shape from the machine. The most modern machines can repeat this process – producing a new component for a model with every cycle – between 80 and 600 times every hour, depending on the number of impressions and the size and weight of the articles. The machines work almost without human supervision. One man, unaided, is kept pleasantly occupied feeding the raw material into six or seven machines!

The question of colour has to be dealt with next. The plastic pellets fed into the machine have been carefully chosen so that the components ejected will have as many surfaces as possible that do not need to be covered with paint. But, there will be almost inevitably some surfaces on each of the models that *do* need some decoration. The prototype may have been (to take a possible example) chocolate brown with yellow enrichments. If that is so, each of the chocolate brown plastic shells will have to proceed to

A technician in the Märklin ...tory testing model locomotives ...at have come off the production ...e.

the spray shop. There, a nimble-fingered repetition-worker will fix it in a specially designed 'jig' with a pierced shield. This shield is to act as a stencil. When quick-drying yellow paint is projected from a compressed-air spray gun at this, in the form of a fine mist, the colour is deposited on the model wherever it is not covered by the shield.

Next, the operatives add any lettering, registration numbers, the railway company's symbols, and other livery markings that are too tiny to be spray-painted through a stencil. A special press has been designed to do this. The press takes a die that has been cut exactly to the shape to be printed on the model. Before the press is operated, the die is heated to a carefully controlled temperature. When the hot metal is pressed on a continuous band of coloured foil, and that, in turn, is pressed against the model, the printing is completed in an operation lasting only a second or two. And, it is much more exact than any that could ever be done by hand.

Fixing the electric motor in position (if the model is a locomotive or a powered diesel or electric-driven unit) is also a matter of seconds. The motor will have been tested carefully at each stage of assembly, but it will be given more, and extremely thorough, running tests before the model passes, finally, to be packed.

Any description of mechanical processes is liable to sound a little prosaic, but there is one department in a well-run railway model factory that could not fail to excite anyone with the smallest streak of romance in his nature. That is the Servicing Department.

Imagine a large, light, airy chamber in which a number of versatile and highly-skilled craftsmen are sitting at conveniently spaced intervals. Their posture – most of them are perched on high stools, with their heels on the upper-side rungs – and their happy and intent expressions make them look like benevolent gnomes. Each has around him a small raised oval of track on which he is able to run under the best possible conditions the models that are allotted to him to mend. Above this magic ring his tools are arranged in tiers, so that he can reach them easily. The tool racks resemble the stands full of spectators that surround the great athletic tracks of the world. They concentrate the attention wonderfully on the small objects that are speeding round each stadium.

At one end of this department there is a long counter at which parcels arrive by the hundred from all corners of the earth. Each of the parcels, when it is unpacked, is found to contain a railway model that has failed to live up to its owner's expectations – that reverses when it is told to advance, or advances when it is told to reverse, or just refuses obstinately to move at all, either way, even if it is kicked.

All too often, there will be no letter in the parcel to say who has sent it. If there is a letter, the writer will probably have omitted to give his – or her – address. Somehow, each model has to be put into proper running order by one of the benevolent gnomes – there is rarely anything wrong, anyway, except an accumulation of fluff – and then it has to be returned, by a combination of the most subtle detective methods and telepathy, to its proper owner, who may, by that time, have actually written: 'Two days ago I sent you a parcel and I forgot . . .'

Above, a Gauge HO9 (narrow gauge) locomotive and rolling stock for quarry working.

Below, a faithful reproduction of the French Paris, Lyons and Mediterranean Railways Pacific locomotive in Gauge HO. This is all metal and unpainted.

5 Truth, Gauges and Scale

The aim of most people who choose to make their own railway models is, quite simply, enjoyment. But most modellers' enjoyment is spoiled if their work does not look right, or true, or if it looks less right or true than the work of their friends. So, we must examine, next, the means by which this correctness may be obtained.

First, the modeller who sets high standards of accuracy has to do a lot of research. It takes much effort to ensure that every detail of an original or 'prototype' is reproduced in a model with one hundred per cent fidelity, but the work has to be done if the model is to be completely convincing. Experts are keen-eyed, and critical, and a model that cannot be faulted is rare, but when one is made or found it can become (as long as its origins are right) like a thing of beauty, a joy for ever. The more handsome the prototype, the more handsome the model – the ultimate results are largely determined by the model-maker's choice of subject.

Normally, perfect accuracy of reproduction can only be obtained by the modeller who is prepared to make an intensive study of the relevant working drawings – often, as we saw when commercial models are being produced, the original working drawings from which the prototype was made, or copies of them – or of photographs, or both. Occasionally, a modeller may be able to get access to the actual prototype, and this is the best possible source of reference, as long as measurements can be taken. As the vast majority of modellers are unable to get this first-hand information, large reference libraries and files of measured drawings and photographs are collected by the officials of the principal model-makers' clubs and societies to help their members to do their homework in a thorough and convenient way. (There are Historical Model Railway Clubs and Societies, or their equivalents, with almost inexhaustible archives, in Great Britain, America, Australia, and several other countries.)

But even the most careful research will be wasted if a modeller neglects to work consistently to a definite scale.

The words 'scale' and 'gauge' are used constantly by all model-makers and model-users who wish their models and layouts to be

ie of the beautiful models made
Bassett-Lowke.

exactly true to life. They are, it would probably be correct to say, the key words of all model railways. So, they must be defined here with some precision.

Gauge we have met already, in the chapter that dealt with commercial model railways. The word is used, in the simplest terms, to establish the track width of a prototype or a model in relation to all other track widths. So, in a real railway system that is classified as 4 feet 8½ inches Gauge or, more easily, as Standard Gauge, the distance between the inner surfaces of the rails will be exactly 4 feet 8½ inches. In a model layout made with a gauge of 2½ inches, the inner surfaces of the rails will be exactly 2½ inches apart.

At this stage, it may be convenient to make a distinction between railway modelling and model railway engineering. To the un-initiated, they may seem quite alike, but they are really very different.

The model engineer is almost invariably a fine craftsman. He tends to build models to a comparatively large scale – models, usually, intended to run on track that has a gauge of 2½ inches or more – 5 inch gauge being particularly popular. His models are usually highly detailed, and each may take many years of hard work to produce. The sheer size of such models is usually enough to exclude them from any miniature railway layout. If they are made to work usefully at all, it is generally to pull live passengers in some outdoor garden system. More often, they finish their

57 Two electrically driven North Eastern Railway Z class 4-4-2 locomotives made by J. Whitwo The upper model is 2½ in. gauge and the lower is in Gauge O.

days as display models in glass cases in museums or private collections.

The railway modeller is a little less exacting. He usually uses track which has an inside width or gauge of $1\frac{3}{4}$ inches (45 millimetres) or less. In models of these smaller sizes one can find many examples of the finest engineering, but it is very difficult to find examples of complete railway systems – with locomotives, coaches, freight cars, station buildings, scenery, and so on – in gauges larger than $1\frac{3}{4}$ inches.

Scale may be defined as the ratio between the size of a model and the size of the prototype or object it represents. Logically, a simple numerical ratio such as 40 : 1 should be enough to explain the relative sizes of the prototype and the model:

Prototype = Forty feet long
Model = One foot long

A further comparison of $2\frac{1}{2}$ in, uge and Gauge O. These models e of the London and North-Western ilway's 0-6-2 tank engine. The iches were made by Bassett- wke in 1910.

But unfortunately, model-makers have not been able to use any system that is quite as straightforward and as easy to understand as that, for Henry Greenly, the original progenitor of the standard model railway gauges, had to face the fact that real life railway lines, or the majority of them, were the awkward distance of 4 feet $8\frac{1}{2}$ inches apart. The matter at once became complicated. The

59 *Left – A gauge N layout bui[lt]*
by C. J. Packham in a violin ca[se]
shows what can be done in a ver[y]
small space.

60 *Below – A diagram to show the*
relationships between the various
'standard' modelling gauges.

61 *Bottom – This live steam mode[l]*
of an Atlantic locomotive was bui[lt]
by W. A. Carter to a scale of $1\frac{1}{16}$
for 5 in. gauge. The boiler is coal-
fired.

62 *Below right – A front view o[f]*
the Atlantic model.

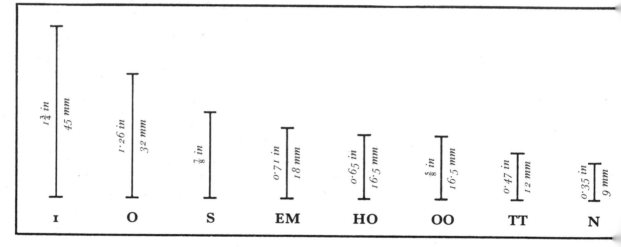

I	O	S	EM	HO	OO	TT	N
$1\frac{3}{4}$ in / 45 mm	1·26 in / 32 mm	$\frac{7}{8}$ in	0·71 in / 18 mm	0·65 in / 16·5 mm	$\frac{5}{8}$ in / 16·5 mm	0·47 in / 12 mm	0·35 in / 9 mm

question of scales, now, can hardly be considered except in relation to the gauges with which they are associated.

Normally, a railway modeller (as opposed to a model railway engineer) chooses a gauge – and, therefore, almost automatically a scale – in a way that reflects his personality and the circumstances under which he has to work. In making his decision, he is usually influenced by his skill (or lack of it), by the amount of space he has available for his model, and by the purpose for which the model is being built. So, a modeller who wishes to show a complete landscape with a railway in it is most likely – all things being equal – to choose a gauge in which the models are made to a small scale (HO, or OO, or even smaller). The skilled scratch-builder who likes every rivet in a model locomotive to be exactly right is more likely to choose a gauge – say, O or 1 – in which the models are made to a larger scale, letting the surroundings of his track play a comparatively minor role. There are examples of freak layouts made – with true-to-scale landscape surroundings – in violin cases, round the brims of hats, on wedding cakes, and in similar strange locations. It has been possible to make these with commercially produced components only because Gauge N – which features models built to a scale of two millimeteres, that is .08 inch (of model) to one foot (of prototype) – has been developed most successfully in recent years by prominent manufacturers.

Although, as has been shown, there is no best scale for railway modellers to work to, some gauges will be found, at any given time, to be more popular than others. These changes of fashion have been found to reflect, in a limited way, changes in social conditions in various parts of the world. Here is a list of the gauges with which, at the present time, the greatest number of railway modellers are likely to be concerned:

Gauge 1 is one of the grand old standard gauges established by Henry Greenly in 1901 and popularized by Wenman Bassett-Lowke. It has a track gauge of 1¾ inches (45 millimetres) and an approximate scale ratio of 30 : 1. It is the largest gauge adopted for railway modelling, as opposed to model railway engineering, and it was at its peak of popularity during the first quarter of the twentieth century when a large proportion of the people who were fortunate enough to be able to buy railway models had homes with big rooms or lofts. Today, when homes tend to be smaller, and more compactly planned, Gauge 1 has a declining appeal, but it still has devoted adherents in all parts of the world. Magnificent models are still being produced in this scale. Gauge 1 is a particularly good choice for outdoor or garden systems and for the experienced live steam modeller. There are few commercial parts available, making it an unsuitable gauge for beginners, who are

recommended to try gauges for which ready-made accessories (castings, wheels, boiler fittings and so on) can be more easily bought.

Gauge O made its appearance quite early in this century. All models made to the new specifications were built to a scale of 7 millimetres, or 0.28 inch (of model) to 1 foot (of prototype), the distance between the inner surfaces of the rails being – this is easy to remember – 32 millimetres, or 1.26 inch. The great German firms of Bing, Carette and Karl Bub were quick to market cheap Gauge O models, few of which had any marked resemblance to any known prototype. This example was soon followed by manufacturers in the United States, working, frequently, to a linear scale of $\frac{1}{4}$ inch (of model) to the foot (of prototype). In Great Britain, Frank Hornby, the man who had invented the ingenious constructional toy known as Meccano, brought out his first clockwork toy trains in Gauge O in the early days of the 1914–18 war, but he had to stop production almost at once because of war restrictions. As soon as he possibly could after the end of hostilities, the energetic Hornby resumed production of his model trains, and soon Gauge O with its scale ratio of 43 : 1 became the standard exhibition railway gauge, many of the world's finest models and layouts being conceived and completed within its limitations.

Gauge OO – made to a scale of 4 millimetres (0.16 inch) of model to 1 foot of prototype: having, that is, a scale ratio of 76 : 1 – was introduced as early as 1913. It received a chilly welcome, largely for social reasons. Nearly everyone who was wealthy enough to afford model railways in those days had enough room to accommodate the grander and more impressive Gauges 1 and O.

Then, in 1921 or 1922, the great German manufacturers, who had been struggling to build up their industry again after the disasters of 1918, introduced a clockwork toy table railway. This, which had a $\frac{5}{8}$ inch gauge track made of lithographed tinplate stampings, with rails, sleepers and ballast all in one piece, was smaller than anything that had been previously placed on the market. Each of the tiny, compact layouts was sold with a London and North Western Railway tank engine, two four-wheeled carriages and a brake van to match. The little trains appeared to run for satisfactorily long distances round curves that were not too sharp and therefore were not unsightly. Models in the new diminutive size had an irresistible appeal for people living in small homes who could not spare the space for Gauge 1 or Gauge O layouts. They sold like wildfire. Before long, amateur craftsmen were making charming little models of their own to this and other miniature scales. The day of the very small gauge had dawned.

63 Above – Gauges O and HO compared. Models of the famous American 4–6–0 locomotive Cas Jones made by Rivarossi.

64 Centre – A model of the Fly Scotsman in front of the Royal Scot. Both models made by Bassett-Lowke in Gauge O.

65 Right – A Southern Railway Tank engine in Gauge OO mad from a Wills 'Finecast' kit of metal parts.

Gauge HO (Half O) was introduced in 1925, or thereabouts. In Great Britain, it was launched with vigour by Wenman Bassett-Lowke, who was quick to see that models made by his firm to the new reduced scale would have at least one distinct advantage over those they had marketed previously: in the smaller models, they could combine a realistic appearance with greater trackage.

Unfortunately for those who find mathematics puzzling, the introduction of Gauge HO brought some confusing factors into a popular hobby that had been up to that time straightforward enough for the average man (or woman) to understand. All HO models are intended to run on track that has a gauge of 16.5 millimetres (0.65 inch), but the manufacturers of the earliest HO models were not so sure about the best linear scale to use on track of this width – the scale ratios 72 : 1, 76 : 1, 80 : 1, 82 : 1 and 90 : 1 were all tried. One can still find a few commercial HO models on sale in these unusual scales, but most American, European and Japanese manufacturers now stick consistently to a scale of 3.5 millimetres (0.14 inch) of model to 1 foot of prototype – that is, a scale ratio of 87 : 1 – which is the correct scale for the gauge. In America, France Germany, Italy, Japan and several other countries HO has become by far the most popular modelling gauge.

Soon after Gauge HO was introduced, some manufacturers in Great Britain who wished to exploit the new gauge commercially ran into some unforeseen difficulties. The generally small size of British prototype locomotives meant that the model locomotives, when made to a scale of 3.5 millimetres (0.14 inch) of model to 1 foot of prototype, were also relatively small – too small, in fact, to accommodate even the smallest electric motor then available. So, those of the British manufacturers who were looking beyond clockwork evolved yet another gauge, which they labelled with the once-tried tag OO. In this, the track gauge was kept at 16.5 millimetres (0.65 inch), but the linear scale was 'stretched' to 4 millimetres of model to 1 foot of prototype (in HO, it will be remembered, the linear scale is 3.5 millimetres to 1 foot). By the time electric motors had been produced that were small enough to be fitted into a Gauge HO model of a British locomotive prototype, the 4 millimetres (0.16 inch): 1 foot scale was too popular and well-established in Britain for there to be any hope of a reversion to HO. The horrible hybrid OO – not HO – is, therefore, one of the most popular gauges in the country of its origin. But as many British OO Gauge models are exported, it is worth remembering that HO and British OO, having the same track gauge, can be run simultaneously on the same layout. (It should be remembered, too, that EM or Eighteen Millimetre (0.71 inch) Gauge, which is almost exclusively British, makes a gallant attempt to obliterate the distortions of OO.)

Two small model trains, commer cially manufactured for narrow gauge working on 9 mm. track.

Overleaf, two live-steam model locomotives made by Bassett-Lo Above, in Gauge 1, a 4–6–0 of th London South Western Railway and below, in Gauge O, a 2–6–0 the London Midland and Scotti Railway.

The next three scales to be described are much 'purer' – that is, more exactly truthful – than the oldest established ratios, in which the gauges were first selected quite arbitrarily in neat fractions of an inch, the linear scales being afterwards chosen to agree with them in a very approximate way.

Gauge S. The gauge known today as S is half the size of Gauge 1 that is, the track gauge is $\frac{7}{8}$ inch, the linear scale is $\frac{3}{16}$ inch of model to each foot of prototype, and the scale ratio is 64 : 1. It was evolved, it is believed, in 1937 by the Cleveland Model and Supply Company. They called it the C–D Gauge, deriving the name from their own Cleveland. Other manufacturers were not so happy about using the name for their own models, since that provided free advertisement for a commercial rival. In preference, they used the clumsy name '$\frac{3}{16}$ inch scale, $\frac{7}{8}$ inch gauge'. Then, Al Kalmbach of the American *Model Railroader* magazine suggested that it should be called S Scale because S stands for sixteenths, seven-eighths and sixty-fourths, all of which are important measurements in the $\frac{3}{16}$ inch scale. In 1943, the members of the American National Model Railroad Association voted at their Convention to make S their official name for the gauge. S is essentially a pure (that is, exact) scratch builder's gauge, and little is available in the way of commercial parts.

Gauge TT also got its name in an unusual way. The letters stand for Table Top. This is how the American HP Products Company advertised, in 1946, models made in TT Scale, which was then quite new:

'TT trim tiny thoroughbred trains travel tracks through tunnels, trestles, turnouts – tugging tiny tons tirelessly towards traffic terminals. Total territory – table top. These thoroughly tested tiny thoroughbreds trundle through towns, thunder through tough territory to the throttle's touch.'

Unfortunately a certain amount of confusion has arisen in TT Gauge, as it has in HO and OO. Some TT models are made commercially in Europe to a linear scale of 3 millimetres (0.12 inch) of model to 1 foot of prototype, which produces a scale ratio of 101 : 1. This is slightly larger than American TT, which has a scale ratio of 120 : 1. In spite of this difference, models from both continents will run quite happily on the same 12 millimetre (0.47 inch) gauge track.

Gauge N layouts, with tracks that have a gauge of 9 millimetres (0.35 inch) only, and tiny trains that move around like busy little

fine scale Gauge O coach and 4–4 tank locomotive built by Major W. Mayhew. The station is once part of the Norris collection.

85

66 Left – Two models of a German Federal Railways locomotive made by Fleischmann; left, in Gauge HO and right, in Gauge N.

67 Below – In Gauge HO, this is a model of an o–3–o tank engine once used in France.

68 Right – a model of a narrow gauge train in G. Grainger's award winning layout of the Milldale line in Yorkshire in Gauge N on HO track.

86

69 A Gauge N model of an Indiana Harbor Belt 0–8–0 locomotive from Atlas.

mice, are now attracting attention in exhibitions and displays in most parts of the world and purchasers, too, in every considerable model shop. The gauge has become, in a rush, one of the most popular of all.

Once more, the birth of a new gauge was accompanied by pangs and upheaval. Gauge N was developed from OOO – a size that was dreamed up in Great Britain to suit railway modellers who have to work in a drastically limited space. OOO models are just half the size of those made for the popular Gauge OO – that is, they are made to a linear scale of 2 millimetres (0.08 inch) of model to 1 foot of prototype. But there are certain disadvantages in this ratio, which perpetuates the 'stretching' error which crept in when electric motors had to be accommodated in the early OO model locomotives.

For a time, American manufacturers followed their British counterparts. Then a slightly smaller version – the present N Scale – was introduced by the German firm of Arnold. Its Rapido line – made with a linear scale of .075 inch of model to 1 foot of prototype and a scale ratio of 160 : 1 – earned high praise from the model railway press, and now MOROP, the organization that looks after the interests of so many European railway modellers, has adopted the proprietary Rapido standards as the correct ones for N Gauge.

Outside the range of gauges between Gauge 1 and N Gauge there are (on the one hand) the really big models that run on tracks with gauges larger than $1\frac{3}{4}$ inches and, at the other end of the range, some beautiful models made to scales as small as 250 : 1. Only a real virtuoso will decide to make models as tiny as that.

The terms Coarse Scale and Fine Scale are used by many railway

modellers. They may be applied to track, or to the wheels of models of any gauge between Gauge 1 (relatively large) and EM (the refined form of Gauge OO). They are sometimes loosely applied, too, to the processes by which the models are produced or to the attitude of the model builder to such matters as detail and proportion. These two usages call for a little explanation.

As we have seen, early commercial models tended to be very crude and had little real resemblance to any known prototype. They had heavy, oversize wheels with clumsy flanges, and they lacked much detail in their superstructure. Although they gave a lot of pleasure to their owners, it was only to be expected that, in time, some non-commercial modellers would wish to get the dimensions of their work closer to correct scale values, and to add much more authentic detail. The idea of modelling to exact proportions in every possible respect, and most especially in respect of the track and wheel contours, originated in Great Britain, where the new approach was called Fine Scale. The term is a misnomer, since the *scale* is not actually changed. In America, the words fine standards or exact standards are usually preferred and give a more accurate idea of the purist modeller's intentions.

In recent years the general standard of commercial models has greatly improved. As a result, potential buyers have been more critical of everything offered them, and inferior and ill-proportioned models have failed to sell. This has lessened the difference between the coarse and fine branches of the hobby until, now, most commercial models built by modern mass-production techniques are far superior to the majority of models built by hand a few years ago. In consequence, there has grown up in recent years a considerable body of enthusiasts who are in the middle of the coarse

71 *Left – A narrow gauge diesel works locomotive modelled by Eggar-Bahn in HO scale using Gauge N track. This is typical of range of narrow gauge equipment manufactured today.*

72 *Below – Another Egger-Bahn narrow gauge locomotive. This scale/gauge is usually written HO9 or HOn9, to indicate that the model is scaled for HO but r on Gauge N (or 9 mm.) track.*

73 & 74 *Opposite – Two views of narrow gauge layout constructed Vic Hart of Warrington. This wo built in the unusual scale of $10\frac{1}{2}$ mm. to 1 ft. The buildings were made of marine plywood.*

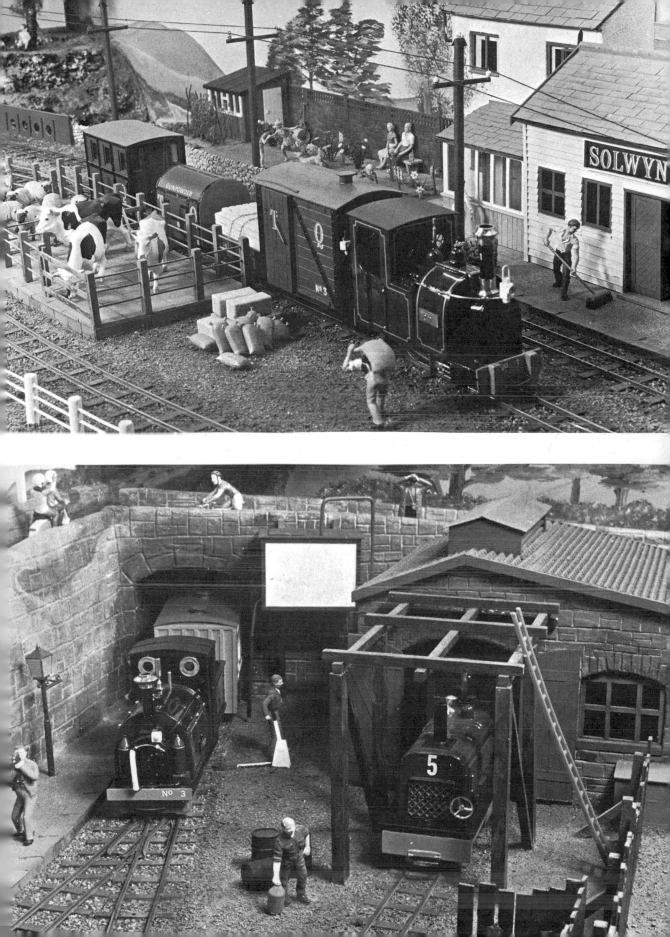

standards/fine standards spectrum. Modellers of this kind make full use of any commercially made parts that may be available, but, in addition, they usually have sufficient skill to be able to fabricate for themselves any items they may need that are not available through the model trade.

One more term needs to be defined – that is, narrow gauge. It is heard frequently, as minor narrow gauge lines are regarded with warm affection by an increasingly large number of modellers.

What *is* narrow gauge?

Standard gauge, in many parts of the world, is 4 feet 8½ inches. In these countries, narrow gauge is, strictly speaking, any prototype gauge that is less wide than this.

But many railroad systems, in other parts of the world, have track that is less than 4 feet 8½ inches wide without being narrow gauge in the generally understood meaning of the words. It is a question of attitude.

In systems of this kind – as, for example, in Malaysia, Tasmania, parts of Switzerland, Spain and Portugal, Japan, South Africa, parts of Australia, parts of India, Indonesia, South Thailand, the Isle of Man, and parts of South America – trains run to more or less exact timetables at express speeds. They are properly signalled and carefully maintained and there is nothing in the slightest amateur or happy-go-lucky about them. These are not true narrow gauge railways, in the modeller's sense, in spite of the narrowness of their track. The people who operate them are as efficient as those connected with any well run standard gauge main line railway.

The true narrow gauge railway has a flavour all its own that the experienced student of railways is quick to recognize.

First, a narrow gauge line will not in any circumstance have any resemblance at all to a normal high speed main line. Any line that carries swift, modern electric or diesel-worked locomotives is disqualified from the narrow gauge modeller's world.

Secondly, the true narrow gauge line is always worked in light railroad fashion – that is, the drivers of the trains that run on it do not bother about signals or time-tables or any other frustrating arrangements of that kind. They are prepared to stop to pick up passengers, or to put them down, not only at the stations along the line, but at any convenient place between.

Thirdly, the locomotives usually have a romantic and slightly old-fashioned look about them, as if they have been left over from some bygone era. Their boilers are often quite small and their chimneys abnormally high, and they carry an amusingly large amount of visible pipework, with primitive accessories, unexplained springs and even a tool-box or two that make them look different. They have the appearance of great age, even though – as in the case of many of them – they were built in the twentieth century.

Above, an all metal model of the famous Bavarian locomotive S 2 in Gauge HO.

Below, model of the 121 Forquen 2–4–2 locomotive in Gauge O, built by P. Lottiaux. The prototype was used in 1878 on the old Paris Orleans Railway.

6 Locomotives and Motorized Units

To many people who devote their working lives or their leisure time to model railways the subject of locomotives is of paramount importance. No part of any system, they feel, is of greater interest than the machines that bring it to life. These people have an enormous field for their researches, since the railways of the world are thronged with steam, diesel and electric locomotives of an almost endless variety. It is an interesting fact that in most languages the word used to describe the immense engines that race across the vast open spaces of the Americas, Australia and Siberia is applied also, without any attempt at distinction, to the little switchers that fuss round freight yards and industrial enterprises, appearing (like so many little men) to have energy and a sense of their own importance wholly disproportionate to their size.

The world's railways depended for more than three-quarters of a century on steam locomotives. Though they are now obsolete in many countries, or are rapidly becoming so, these locomotives, developed from the comparatively crude experimental engines of Trevithick and Stephenson, have a compulsive fascination for a great many of the railway enthusiasts who are clever enough to be able to make their own models, and obstinate enough to insist on continuing to do so. This interest is understandable, as a large proportion of these craftsmen have been trained as engineers, and are therefore able to appreciate the splendid ingenuity and the feeling for the finer points of design that characterized the work of their steam age predecessors.

Today, the railways of the world provide such a safe form of travel that it is salutary to recall some of the dangerous weaknesses that had to be overcome by the designers of the earlier steam locomotives. One of the more regrettable characteristics of these hissing, puffing iron beasts was their tendency to blow up. The passengers would settle themselves trustfully in their seats at the start of a journey, hoping that the boiler of the engine that was taking them would not burst before they reached their destination, but they had no real confidence in their chances of survival. Their fears can be readily appreciated. Once locomotives had passed into service at that time they were only infrequently inspected if they

lose up of the pantograph on a del of a Swiss electric locomotive.

95

were at all, and to make matters worse the Salter-type safety valves that were fitted then were not infallible. On engines that had little reserve of power and were often expected to draw impossibly heavy burdens these valves could be all too easily screwed down by unscrupulous engine drivers until they provided no protection whatsoever.

As the nineteenth century passed, the relatively simple forms of the earliest steam locomotives were developed until there were a large number of distinct types, each designed to suit a particular set of conditions or to perform a particular kind of service.

First, the designer of a locomotive had to make a number of calculations to ensure that the finished engine would be heavy enough to be stable and yet light enough to travel safely at any foreseeable speed over the existing, or projected, tracks, viaducts and bridges. (These calculations were not always carried out correctly. The history of the early railways is freely punctuated with accounts of accidents caused by breakage and earth subsidence, many lives being lost when passengers were plunged without warning from inadequate structures into rivers, lakes and several other natural hazards.)

Then, the designer had to ensure that his locomotive would be narrow enough and low enough to clear all tunnel and cutting surfaces, station platforms, and other possible obstacles. He had to see that it would be powerful enough to cope with all the gradients it would be likely to meet, and that it would be able to negotiate without leaving the rails even the sharpest curves in the tracks over which it could possibly run. He had to guarantee that it would be fast enough to conform to its sponsoring company's schedules (and where competition was fierce, these could be exacting). He had to arrange for it to carry enough fuel and water to take it over the longest possible distance between supply stations. (The impressively elongated form of the locomotives intended to draw the great American expresses is due largely to the vast, unpopulated expanses of land these trains were intended to span.) He had to be sure that it would be able to draw a certain specified load. With all these factors to consider, it is not surprising that steam railway designers produced locomotives in a variety that is, to all but a few scholarly experts, slightly bewildering.

To help people to differentiate between the various types of steam locomotive, certain classifications have been evolved. First, they may be generally divided into two main categories:

TENDER ENGINES, which have a separate carriage or 'tender' for their fuel and water.

TANK ENGINES, which are self-contained locomotives, with the water tank or tanks and fuel bunkers all placed in a single frame.

75 Above – A Rivarossi HO model of an 0–6–0 tender engine used on French National Railw

76 Centre – A diesel switcher in Gauge HO of Japanese Nationa Railways. The wheel configurat is Bo–Bo.

77 Right – A Märklin model of electric locomotive – the Capito in Gauge HO, showing the two pantographs.

Tender engines were designed for drawing long distance passenger or freight trains; tank engines were designed for short-run passenger, local freight and shunting purposes.

These two main categories may be further sub-divided. The system generally followed is that devised by F. M. Whyte, Mechanical Engineer of the New York Central and Hudson River Railroad Company. In Whyte's system, numbers are used to indicate the locomotive's wheel arrangement. A locomotive (or model locomotive) may be described, for instance, as a 4–8–2 type. To translate this into terms that a layman can understand, one has to know that:

The first numeral represents the number of wheels in the pilot, or leading, truck.

The second numeral represents the number of driving wheels.

The third numeral represents the number of wheels in the rear or trailing truck.

So, the locomotive in question would have four pilot wheels, eight driving wheels, and two trailing wheels.

When a locomotive has more than one set of driving wheels, the classification is normally made up of four numerals instead of three, the second and third representing the two driving sets. (The engines in the 4000 class of the Union Pacific Railway, which had a 4–8–8–4 wheel arrangement, were the largest steam locomotives ever built. Each of these engines, with its fourteen-wheeled tender, weighed 539 tons.)

In some parts of Europe a system of classification similar to Whyte's is in use, axles being counted instead of wheels. An American 4–4–2 locomotive would, in this system, be known as a 2–2–1.

But numerals, however useful for conveying factual information, are not very glamorous, and inevitably the most commonly encountered types of locomotive have been given at various times their own individual names, the best known of these being:

The *American* (4–4–0) type, which got its name because passenger locomotives with this wheel arrangement were more widely used than any others on American railroads during the nineteenth century. Rivarossi have marketed a handsome exact-scale reproduction of the 4–4–0 Genoa locomotive built in 1873 by Baldwin of Philadelphia for the Virginia and Truckee Railroad.

The *Atlantic* (4–4–2) type, called so because the first prototypes with this wheel arrangement were constructed for the Atlantic Coast Line. The *Atlantic* may be regarded as a development of

78 Above – Model of a London Midland and Scottish Railway 2–6–4 tank in Gauge OO.

79 Centre – A ½ in. scale model of the New York Central Hudson 4–6–4 tender locomotive.

80 Right – Two 0–6–0 tender locomotives of the Midland Railway shown on part of the Derby Model Railway layout. (Gauge O).

1 *Left above – A Great Northern railway 4–8–4 tender locomotive modelled in Japan.*

2 *Left centre – The Bassett-Lowke model of the 4–6–2 Coronation.*

3 *Left below – 4–6–0 The Royal Artilleryman modelled by K. Longbottom.*

4 *Right above – A Japanese-made model of a 2–8–0 locomotive used on the Great Northern Railway.*

5 *Right centre – Also Japanese made, this model is of the Canadian Pacific Railways 4–6–0 Royal Hudson.*

6 *Right – The* Casey Jones *– a 4–6–0 locomotive made by Rivarossi.*

the 4–2–2 type. Having coupled driving wheels, which could be of moderate size, the new locomotives had a real advantage over the older engines, which in certain cases had driving wheels that were over 8 feet in diameter, tread to tread.

The *Consolidation* (2–8–0) type. Found so generally useful that (among relatively recent examples) twenty-five formidable outside-cylinder goods locomotives with this wheel arrangement were made by the North British Locomotive Company for the East Indian Railways in 1923. The tender of each of the locomotives, on two four-wheeled bogies, carried 4,500 gallons of water and ten tons of coal.

The *Mikado* (2–8–2) type. The first *Mikado* locomotives were built for Japanese railroads.

The *Pacific* (4–6–2) type – given this name, because early loco-motives with this wheel arrangement were made for the Canadian Pacific Railways and for the New Zealand railway systems, being shipped to New Zealand from the United States across the Pacific Ocean. More recent examples have been the Chapelon 4–6–2s used on the Paris–Orleans–Midi Railway, and the famous three-cylinder *Flying Scotsman* that is warmly admired by so many British railway modellers. Designed by Sir Nigel Gresley, this was the first of its class to attain a speed of 100 miles per hour.

The *Prairie* (2–6–2) type. Some of the most generally useful steam locomotives had a 2–6–2 wheel arrangement.

The *Ten Wheeler* (4–6–0) type, developed from the 4–4–0 type to provide more adhesion, and greater steam raising facilities.

87 A ½ in. scale model of the United Pacific Big Boy in the Smithsonian Institution. The wheel configuration is 4–8–8–4.

For the heaviest express passenger work in the United States, the 4–8–4 type has been often adopted. Among the most impressive locomotives with this wheel arrangement were those in the 3776 class of the Atchison, Topeka and Santa Fé Railroad. These engines worked regularly over the 1,788 miles between Los Angeles and Kansas City, being manned by twelve different crews in turn. Each had a tractive effort of 66,000 pounds.

Inevitably, with so many different designers commissioned to produce steam locomotives in so many different parts of the world to suit such various conditions, there will have been some types of engine that have proved to be outstandingly successful, and others that have turned out to be expensive and even disastrous failures. One ill-conceived project produced the locomotive *Great Bear*. This was built at the Swindon Works in 1908 to the designs of George Jackson Churchward, and was the first tender engine of the Pacific type to be tried in Great Britain. It turned out that, owing to its enormous size and weight, the *Great Bear* could only be used satisfactorily for runs between the two terminal cities of London and Bristol. When later research showed that much smaller boilers could supply adequate steam for four 15-inch cylinders, no further engines of the type were built at Swindon.

The decline and fall of the steam locomotive – which would have been inevitable, anyway, once the full resources of electric power had been made available – were hastened by the invention of the diesel engine. In some parts of the world – notably, South Africa, where the coal is both excellent and relatively cheap – the steam locomotive has lingered on, but there are few countries now that have steam operated systems and fully intend to keep them.

It was the German engineer and inventor Rudolf Diesel who, in 1892, patented the first internal combustion engine of the type that now bears his name. (A British engineer, Herbert Ackroyd-Stuart, had taken out patents some years earlier that covered certain improvements to oil engines, but Diesel is generally given the credit for the discovery.)

The diesel engine is designed to exploit the fact that when air is compressed its temperature rises. In a normal commercial diesel engine air is compressed (either by an auxiliary motor or an electric dynamo) to about 500 pounds per square inch. This raises its temperature to about 1000°F, which is higher than the flash point of diesel gas. When a spray of diesel oil is injected into the heated air it becomes volatile, and explodes, setting the engine in motion. There is no need, in a diesel engine, for a sparking plug, as there is in a petrol engine.

In countries where oil was readily available in considerable quantities, the advantages of the diesel engine soon became apparent. (Many railroads in the west and middle west of the United States had, in fact, switched almost entirely to oil-fired steam locomotives, even before the general swing towards diesel engines began during the Second World War.) Today, diesel-electric and diesel-hydraulic locomotives are ordered for most non-electrified lines.

Diesel locomotives are not classified in the same way as steam locomotives. In the later system of classification, the letters of the alphabet are used, as well as numbers. The letters denote axles which are driven by a motor:

A means one driving axle, with two wheels
B means two driving axles, with four wheels
C means three driving axles, with six wheels
D means four driving axles, with eight wheels

Numbers are used to denote axles that are not connected to a motor:

1 means one free-running axle with two wheels

So, a diesel locomotive classified as A1A–A1A will have one driving axle, one free running axle and one driving axle (in that order) at each end of the locomotive.

Where each axle is driven by a motor, a small letter o is added. So, a Bo–Bo diesel locomotive will have two axles at each end, all the axles being motor-driven.

A hyphen or dash is used to divide groups of axles that are mounted on separate wheelbases (as in A1A–A1A and Bo–Bo, above). The dash is replaced by a + sign when an articulated joint links the wheel groups together.

88 Above left – A model of a light industrial diesel engine made by Tyco in Union Pacific livery.

89 Above right – A model of a diesel locomotive of the French National Railways, Bo–Bo, made by Au Pullman.

90 Right – A layout owned by M. Hauvette showing an electric freight train. The model draws its power from the overhead wire system just as does the prototype

Surprisingly, the smaller diesel locomotives used merely for shunting are classified by the older system evolved for steam locomotives!

Diesel-electric locomotives made to a manufacturer's standard design are often arranged to be coupled in multiple, so that one may see one, two, three or even more units working together, to suit the needs of a particular train load. The manufacturers of commercial railway models usually offer their miniature diesel units in pairs – one of the units being, in practice, motorised; the other being a non-powered dummy. Together, the two units represent the back-to-back double heading that is now so familiar a sight on the prototype railroads of the Western Hemisphere.

In some European countries, diesel locomotives have been introduced to perform duties formerly carried out by steam engines, but the general trend has been in another direction. Most of the railways in Austria, Belgium, France, The Netherlands and Switzerland are now operated electrically, steam locomotives having almost entirely disappeared from the principal systems of those countries.

Most modern systems of electrification involve the use of a third rail, at ground level, as in the Southern Region of British Railways, or an overhead wire system known as a catenary. Each engine designed to work from a catenary has to have a framework called a pantograph attached to its roof, and this can be raised by the driver until it presses against the overhead contact wire. The current from the contact wire passes down the pantograph to the electric motor in the train. When it leaves the motor, it usually returns to a sub-station, to complete the circuit, by way of the wheels and the running rails.

The systems of overhead supply vary from country to country:

The Netherlands, and parts of France: 1500 volts, direct current.
Belgium and Italy: 3000 volts, direct current.
Austria, Germany and Switzerland: 15,000 volts, alternating current.
Great Britain (in all regions but Southern) and in all new installations in France: 25,000 volts, alternating current, fifty cycles.

Locomotives are now being designed that can be operated on any, or all, of the four main systems. These locomotives are fitted with adaptors that enable them to change quickly and easily from any one system to any of the others, and to be able to do this repeatedly in the course of a single journey.

The new high speed diesel and electric locomotives do not commend themselves to all railway enthusiasts who make their own models or to the people who collect those that have already been hand-built, even in the countries where the prototypes are mainly

*Fleischmann have modelled this
-Co diesel locomotive; the proto
e is used on Belgian National
ilways.*

of these kinds. The austere and strictly functional shapes of the latest units and motorised cars may hide superlatively designed equipment that enables phenomenal power to be developed at the touch of a finger, but when the whole machine is scaled down to a tiny fraction of its original size it is the outside appearance of the prototype, rather than the engineering of its inner workings, that matters most to craftsmen and collectors who have keen eyes for the picturesque. There are no diesel or electric locomotives so far, these connoisseurs claim, that have the extraordinary aesthetic appeal of the great steam engines shown in these pages, with their highly individual styles and their fascinating array of external gadgets.

With the passing of the years and the completion of many long-term schemes of modernisation, tastes will inevitably change, though the memory of steam may be, as King Charles II of Great Britain said of himself in his last sickness, 'an unconscionable time dying'. Predictably, the effects of the new aesthetic will be felt first in the field of commercial model railways, where the production of miniature 'steam' locomotives has for some time past been regarded as an operation aimed at a nostalgic and therefore dwindling market. Already, a directive has gone out to the forward-planning executives of one of the world's principal railway model producing companies. 'Forget about steam', this bit of paperwork said with brutal clarity, 'instead concentrate on diesel and electricity. They are going to be our bread and butter from now on.'

The shift of emphasis may be regrettable – what would Trevithick and the Stephensons have thought of those words 'Forget about steam'? – but commercial model railways, like the real railways on which they are based, have to keep up with the times. That way lies not only bread and butter, but also champagne.

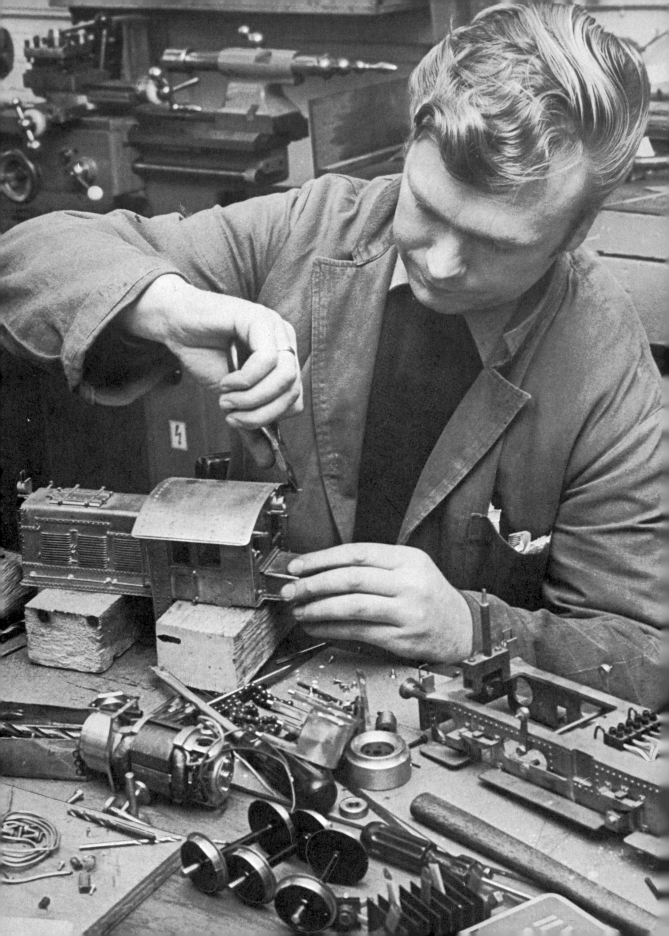

7 Making Model Locomotives

Today, when there are so many great firms like Märklin, Athearn Inc, LIMA, Rivarossi and Fleischmann offering superbly detailed true-to-scale model locomotives at prices well within the reach of the average wage earner, there would seem to be little point in including in this book a chapter that deals mainly with making model locomotives at home, or in the home workshop. But commercially made models do not have a universal appeal. There are many enthusiasts who would only grudgingly give room on their tracks to 'bought' locomotives. Model-lovers of this kind may seem to have masochistic self-torturing tendencies to those who are inclined to take the easier way, but (whatever their motivations) they find real fulfilment only in the exercise of their own skill and ingenuity. So, no review of the world of model railways would be complete without a proper tribute to the tenacity of the amateur craftsmen who insist on making their own replicas of the great locomotives of the past and present, even in an age of mass-production. These men are working honourably in the traditions of the steam age pioneers.

To get some order into this survey, it may be useful to divide those who make model locomotives by hand into three separate categories – those, usually the young, who get their first introduction to personal model-making by being offered ready-to-assemble kits; the more skilful, who are able to use lathes, power drills and other workshop tools, but who do not hesitate to incorporate commercially made motors, bearings, wheels, gears, couplers and other fittings in their work; and the consummate craftsmen who can build from scratch excellent replicas of superlative prototypes without using any commercially-made parts at all. As a further refinement, the model-makers who feel compelled to construct their own miniature locomotives can also be sub-divided into two additional categories – those who get the greatest part of their pleasure from making and assembling the various components of a model, and from enjoying its finished appearance; and those who are only really happy when they see the models they have made actually operating as the original prototypes worked. Of all these categories, it seems logical to begin with the most elementary.

A young technician making a model diesel locomotive for the Madurodam layout in The Hague.

The construction of a model locomotive from a modern proprietary kit is normally a simple and straightforward job. Except in the case of the most refined kits, intended only for experts, few tools are needed – only, perhaps, a small file or sharp knife and a pair of pliers, with, possibly, a small drill that can be used for making holes for fixing handrail knobs and other appendages. In most kits, the parts are designed to interlock with the parts that adjoin them, and are held in place with balsa cement, or some resin-based adhesive recommended by the manufacturer. (If the components are clamped carefully together and held a foot or so away from a 1 kilowatt fan heater the bonding agent will normally be found to have started to cure within ten minutes, and it will be quite hard in less than half an hour.) As only high quality alloys are used in the majority of kits made of metal, good joints can be produced without the use of solder.

An increasing number of kits, today, are being made with plastic instead of metal parts, since these are undoubtedly easier to put together. The assembly of plastic kits is usually carried out with specially recommended plastic cements such as butyl acetate. These cements bring about a complete fusion of the adjoining parts, bonding them to each other without the use of heat as inseparably as if they were actually welded together.

A model locomotive made from a kit will resemble the prototype more or less exactly only if the manufacturer has taken the necessary trouble to make his wares authentic. If he has (and this is highly probable, since kits whose models do not closely resemble their prototype tend not to sell) it will be up to the person assembling the kit to finish off a good job by painting the model with care.

There are, broadly speaking, two methods of giving a model locomotive made from a kit its correct livery – with oil or synthetic paints applied with soft brushes, or with cellulose paints applied through a spray. Most modellers apply a basic coat of black or grey, first. Then, when this initial coat has hardened, they mask off the parts of the surface that are to remain black (or grey), and they brush or spray colour on the exposed areas. Lining can be carried out with a draughtsman's bow pen, loaded with paint, and guided by a straight edge.

Most modellers who decide to make their own locomotives – instead of relying on commercially produced kits – are faced with the problem of finding sufficient information to be able to build satisfactory replicas of their chosen prototypes. In some cases, the firms that made the original locomotives will supply dimensioned drawings, or photostat copies of them. If the firm no longer exists, the necessary information can often be obtained from the reference sections of the leading model-makers' clubs, or from the model railway press, in which excellent line drawings are published from

Bill Banwell at his modelling ben on which so many reproductions of London North Eastern Railwa locomotives have been made.

time to time. If no other sources of information are available, reasonably accurate model locomotives can be made, at a pinch, from photographs alone. (For this to be possible, the photographs have to be taken squarely on at the midpoint of the locomotive, and at least one key dimension – such as the distance between a pair of wheel centres – must be known.)

Not all the clever craftsmen who make model locomotives are keen on working exactly to a prototype. Some get an immense amount of pleasure from designing model locomotives to suit their own personal specifications – to satisfy, possibly, some hidden or unacknowledged creative urges that have found no other outlet. Unfortunately, few of these men who have so much initiative have enough knowledge of the basic principles of railway engineering to make a success of the venture, and their activities – known usually as free-lance model locomotive making – are often cruelly ridiculed by the members of the strict-replica school.

It would be impossible to make an exact list of the tools that a normally skilled model-maker will need for building locomotives, since there are many different ways of carrying out each operation, but there are a few tools that are almost indispensable if the creative process is not to be merely a rough piece of handiwork.

First, the model-maker needs some implements for marking out his components with a high degree of accuracy. A typical marking-out kit might include a scriber (for drawing lines on metal or plastic), a steel ruler (for measuring, and for use as a straight edge), a metal square (for drawing right angles exactly), and a pair of engineers' dividers.

For cutting out the components and giving them an exact shape, most model-makers elect to use a piercing saw, fitted with the finest blades. Swiss files – knife-edged, flat and round – are almost universally popular.

Not many amateur model-makers are able to afford to equip an extensive machine shop for their hobby, or have had sufficient training and experience to get the best possible results from one if they can. Without (say) a centre lathe, a milling machine, a bench grinder and a vertical drill even a skilled engineer has little chance of producing one of the splendid models, each of which has an almost incredible amount of power in relation to its size, that draw such large crowds – and win so many trophies – at all the major exhibitions. Fortunately, though, no one who has to work within relatively modest limitations need be deterred from setting out to build working locomotives to quite a high standard of appearance and performance. The pleasure and satisfaction that can be gained from model-making does not go in direct proportion to public acclaim.

The materials most commonly used by non-commercial makers

exact replica in miniature of Rocket. *This solid silver and wood model was made by Dr. J. adbury Winter, assisted by Miss istabel Mackworth.*

93 *A kit of parts in plastic and metal from Märklin.*

94 *Below – A completed model of an electric locomotive made from a similar kit.*

95 *Right – Three stages in the construction of a 'Finecast' mode of a tank locomotive from a kit cast metal parts. Such kits are often designed to fit a proprietar chassis.*

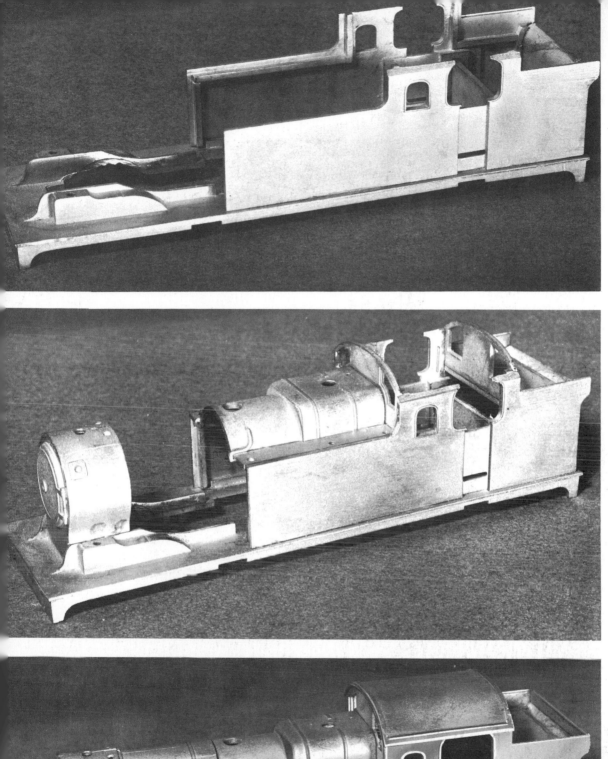
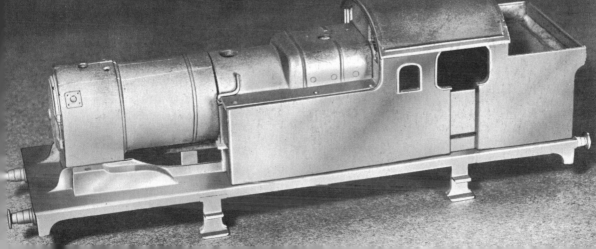

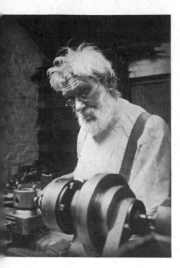

6 Left – A close-up of the cab of the Atlantic live steam locomotive illustrated on page 76, showing the amount of detail achieved by a meticulous craftsman.

7 Above – A Bassett Lowke craftsman working at a lathe at the beginning of the century.

of model locomotives are nickel silver, brass, copper and tinplate – that is, tin-coated mild steel. Nickel silver can be obtained in rods, bars and sheets of various thicknesses (sheets .001 inch thick being particularly useful for platework). When a length of brass or copper tube is to be used for making the boiler of a steam locomotive, careful modellers check that the tube has been made by being drawn, and is therefore seamless. Jointed tubes may have concealed weaknesses that are liable to cause disturbing – and possibly dangerous – blow-outs when steam pressure is raised.

Gold and silver are more precious metals that have been occasionally used for making model locomotives. The great Italian firm of Rivarossi has temptingly offered some beautiful gold-plated models, but these have tended, understandably, to be rather expensive. Lionel, the United States firm, made up a number of gondola cars in gold and other colours in 1950 for use on special display stands arranged for dealers who were to extol the advantages of Maine Traction.

More historically, there is in the Great Western Railway Museum, at Swindon, in Great Britain, a six-wheeled silver-plated model locomotive of singular quaintness and charm, named after the long-reigning British monarch Queen Victoria. Decorated with crowns, lions and other emblems of imperial power, it was made by a firm of jewellers and silversmiths established at Cheltenham, Gloucestershire, to serve as a coffee container in Swindon Station's refreshment room. Unfortunately, the coffee that this magnificent urn dispensed was almost undrinkable. It drove the great engineer Isambard Kingdom Brunel to complain bitterly to the proprietor of the refreshment room:

Dear Sir,
I assure you Mr. Player was wrong in supposing that I thought you purchased inferior coffee. I thought I said to him I was surprised you should buy such bad roasted corn. I did not believe you had such a thing as coffee in the place; I am certain I never tasted any. I have long ceased to make complaints at Swindon. I avoid taking anything there when I can help it.
Yours faithfully,
I. K. BRUNEL

A model of the Stephensons' great award-winning locomotive *Rocket* made almost entirely from sterling silver can be seen at the Institution of Mechanical Engineers in Birdcage Walk, London. The famous craftsman Doctor Bradbury Winter was commissioned to make this model by the members of the Institution in 1930. Of all the parts, only two struts are not made of silver – they, for strength, had to be made of stainless steel.

98 The model of the Stephensons' Rocket *made by Dr Bradbury Winter in sterling silver for the Institution of Mechanical Engineers in London. The boiler and two views of the chassis are shown. See also the plate on p . 1*

In his working hours, Doctor Winter was a prominent surgeon at Brighton, on the South Coast. Like many men who bear special responsibilities, the Doctor needed periods of complete relaxation, so he found relief from the anxieties of the operating table in the inanimate problems of the workbench. He enjoyed making clocks, and he enjoyed making models with metal, and most of all he enjoyed contriving secret locks and security devices.

At the time of his life when he was invited to make the model of the *Rocket* for the Institution, Doctor Winter had been advised to go to Switzerland for the sake of his health. So, he took a small building in the mountains, inviting his niece, who had been acting as his nurse and surgical mechanic, to accompany him as his house-keeper and assistant. There, in the clean mountain air, where the silver with which he was working was less likely to become tarnished than in murky old England, he made the model that proved to be his masterpiece. His particular ingenuity found a proper outlet in the model's casing. Only someone who knows the secret can open the case, and only someone who can find and open a carefully concealed panel can operate the model.

If gold and silver are materials that are likely to be chosen only by comparatively wealthy model-makers, or those who are working for wealthy patrons, styrene, a cheap plastic material that has been developed and marketed only in recent years, is appealing increasingly to those with strictly limited means. Styrene is easily worked – a razor saw, a sharp knife, some small drills and two or three fine files are the only tools needed for cutting and shaping it. As with plastic kits, liquid solvents are sold that will join pieces of styrene quickly, easily and almost inseparably.

Joining pieces of nickel silver, brass, copper, tinplate and other metals is not such an easy job. Most model-makers who are skilful enough to make some at least of their own parts from metal find it best to learn how to use solder successfully. Various techniques are recommended, but among the conditions that must be fulfilled before any technique can be wholly successful there are some that are common to all soldering methods – the parts to be joined must be quite clean and free from grease; the soldering iron that is to supply the necessary heat must be brought to, and kept at, the right temperature for the solder that is being used; and a suitable flux (or material to aid the flow of the solder) must be used in conjunction with the solder and the heated iron. Some model-makers find that a dentist's drill, fitted with a fine burr, is extremely useful for clearing away odd tears of unwanted solder from inaccessible places once the joining operation is over.

Although adhesive cements can be used for joining parts of plastic models, and solder can be used for joining metal, some thought has to be given by the model-maker to the way in which the

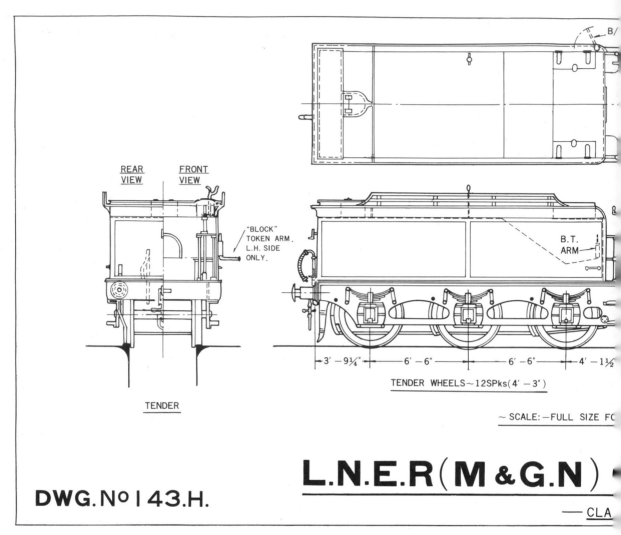

REAR VIEW FRONT VIEW

"BLOCK" TOKEN ARM. L.H. SIDE ONLY.

B.T. ARM

←— 3' — 9¼" —→←——— 6' — 6" ———→←——— 6' — 6" ———→←— 4' — 1½

TENDER WHEELS ~ 12 SPks (4' — 3")

~ SCALE: — FULL SIZE FC

TENDER

L.N.E.R (M & G.N)

DWG. Nº 143. H.

— CLA

various parts of the prototype were actually joined. Rivets have been widely used in railway workshops, ever since the earliest days of locomotive construction. They have been largely superseded now by welding processes, but in their time they were preferred to bolts and studs because the actual operation of riveting caused the rivets to expand so that they plugged tightly the holes through which they passed. They were useful, therefore, for making water-tight and steam-tight joints in boilers and tanks and as they had no nuts to work loose they were relatively accident-proof.

While a few railway engineers of the pre-welding era delighted in the smooth, gleaming surfaces of their locomotives, and used countersunk rivets, carefully finished flush with the surrounding metal, to preserve these, other engineers – Webb, Churchward, and many more – preferred to use snap-head rivets. When these rivets were fitted snugly in place they showed, proud of the surface, their high domed heads. They were usually arranged carefully in

99 A reproduction of a blueprint typically used by model makers. Further help would be derived from the use of photographs of th prototype engine.

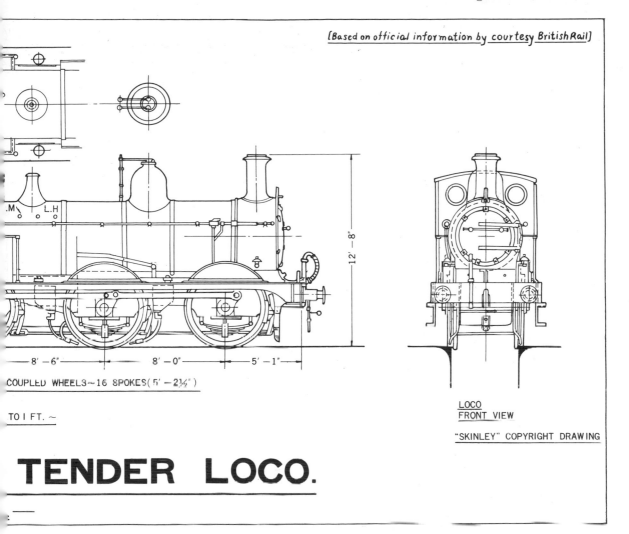

[Based on official information by courtesy British Rail]

12' — 8"

— 8' — 6" —   — 8' — 0" —   — 5' —1" —

COUPLED WHEELS ~ 16 SPOKES (5' — 2¼")

TO I FT. ~

LOCO
FRONT VIEW

"SKINLEY" COPYRIGHT DRAWING

TENDER LOCO.

straight lines on the outer surfaces of the locomotives and tenders on which they were used, resembling so many rigidly regimented pimples. (One writer has pointed out, acutely, that it was often the spottiest locomotives that had the most romantic and exotic names, such as *Fire Queen* and *Lady of Shallott*.)

Model-makers intent on reproducing locomotives that are, or were, plentifully supplied with snap-head rivets have often found that the small entomological pins used by naturalists to impale insects and other victims are admirably suited to represent miniature rivets. The pins, which are made of brass, and are either plated or black enamelled, are inserted in small holes made with a tiny electric drill. If the right size of pin is chosen, the final effect is remarkably realistic.

It is often assumed, in railway modelling circles, that standards of craftsmanship are being progressively lowered, that there are few engineers, if there are any at all, still capable of building model

locomotives to the same degree of exactness as those on view in the Smithsonian Institution in Washington, the Science Museum in London, the Museum of Swiss Transport at Lucerne, to name only three places where superb examples of railway model engineering are on view.

This assumption is wrong. One has only to visit the workshops attached to these museums to see busy men who are as highly trained, as painstaking, and as resourceful as any of the engineers employed by Wenman Bassett-Lowke in the early years of this century.

There are many clever men, too, on the staffs of the companies of specialist model-makers – the firms that supply the leading railway companies of the world, for prestige purposes, with replicas of their latest locomotives – producing the models, frequently, even before the prototypes have made their first appearances on public tracks.

The most remarkable, possibly, of all, because they are unpaid, are the austere and devoted amateur model engineers who come together at quiet and unpublicized rallies to show off their favourite engines ('I have been working on it for fifteen years so far, and it isn't finished yet'); to criticize those of their rivals ('If you ask me, it's just doctored Bassett-Lowke'); and to see both the despised and admired vie with each other on strictly neutral track.

These gatherings are serious, even scholarly occasions. They are attended by the mature and the conservative, rather than by the young and the progressive, and the participants will often look disapprovingly at mere striplings of fifty or sixty years old

100 A 5 in. gauge model, made for the Science Museum in London, of the British Railways Deltic class diesel-electric.

who unthinkingly introduce unwanted modern ideas. (A novice at a recent 'live steam' rally who brought water for his locomotive in a washed-out plastic detergent container instead of an orthodox metal can was treated with chilly reserve.)

But the ancients, though so reluctant to alter their ideas to suit contemporary pressures, are generally extremely sensitive to change – that is, as long as it is change that affects their beloved prototypes. They collect and barter photographs avidly, gazing into fading prints with powerful magnifying glasses in their dim-eyed attempts to see whether any modifications have been made, since the original working drawings were prepared, to the loco-motives they have modelled – whether tool boxes, or any other accessories have been added, tanks moved or patched, or linings altered or removed altogether. The most meticulous craftsmen will guarantee each of their locomotives to be absolutely correct to prototype, down to the very last rivet – and correct, that is, as it was on one particular, specified day in its history.

With so venerable a membership, it would be easy to assume that each of these groups has a brief and temporary existence. But life is rarely as simple as that. Virtue, like Nature, has a miraculous capacity for renewing itself. As the older members of these organizations fade away and disappear, new recruits seem to come, apparently from nowhere, to slip quietly and unobtrusively into the places of those who have cleaned their machines down for the very last time. While men as skilled and industrious as these can still be found in the world of small scale railways, the age of great model engineers cannot be said to be over.

1 An engineer in the Märklin factory making a die.

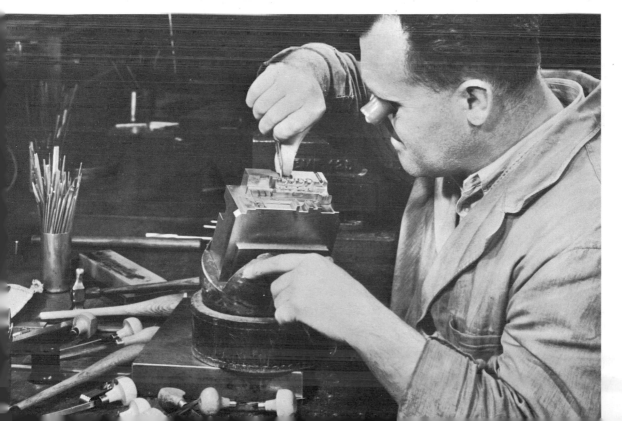

8 Clockwork, Friction, Steam and Electricity

To many of the people who love model railways, a train that will not move is of relatively little interest. If the prime function of the prototype is to carry passengers or freight from one place to another, these enthusiasts ask, of what value to anyone is a static replica? Other people – notably, the collectors of fine old engines – prefer non-operating models, with their original finish in a fine state, to models that run, and show, in consequence, the inevitable signs of wear and tear.

Up to now, there have been four principal ways of inducing model trains to move in a more or less realistic manner: clockwork, by friction, by steam, and by electricity. The advantages of the last method are rapidly making it the universal favourite, but clockwork and steam have long and honourable histories.

Nobody knows exactly who first introduced the ancient principles of clockwork into the construction of model locomotives, but it is likely that the earliest spring-powered toy trains were those made by George W. Brown and Company of Forestville, Connecticut, in the United States, and first marketed in 1856. At that time, Bristol, Connecticut, of which Forestville forms a part, was an important clock-making centre, and Brown was one of the leading manufacturers. Soon, Brown met competition from Messrs Ives of Bridgeport, Althof, Bergmann, and several other firms. Today, collectors of early mechanical models search eagerly for the clockwork locomotives made by Ives, many of which were fitted with working air whistles, cigarette-burning devices that sent smoke puffing realistically from the smoke stacks, and other novel features.

Commercial clockwork trains were first introduced in Europe by the brothers Märklin who, as has already been described, caused a sensation with the toy sets they showed at the Leipzig Spring Fair of 1891. The first true-to-scale models that incorporated clockwork mechanisms followed shortly after. One of the finest of these resulted from a partnership formed by Doctor Bradbury Winter (later, to make the silver model of the *Rocket* described in Chapter 7) with a Doctor Covenden who lived in the same town. In 1895, or thereabouts, the two doctors produced a

2 Above – With a gauge of mm. this clockwork train was made in Germany about 1920.

3 Left – The first Bassett-Lowke clockwork locomotive – a model of the Peckett saddle-tank. This was manufactured about 1906.

Gauge O model railway based on local prototypes, the locomotives of which were most efficiently driven by clockwork. Resourcefully, the doctors fitted a clockwork engine in one of their painted cardboard carriages so that this could be used to boost the power of the clockwork engines.

Wenman Bassett-Lowke was soon to follow Doctor Bradbury Winter's example. Impressed by the comparatively crude German models he had seen at the Paris Exhibition of 1900, the Northampton engineer brought out in 1904 the first true-to-prototype commercial clockwork locomotives – a Great Western Atbara Class 4–4–0 express engine, in Gauges O and 1, and a Gauge O model of the Saddle Tank locomotive designed by Messrs Pecketts of Bristol. The Peckett tank model, which was fitted with machine cut gears throughout and could reverse, remained a popular Bassett-Lowke line until 1914.

Until the outbreak of the First World War, there was much exchanging of ideas between the British and the German firms, and clockwork engines of some quality were produced in both countries and sold in very large numbers. Unfortunately for serious model-owners, clockwork had become by that time the motive element in a large number of nursery toys, and this exposed adult users of clockwork-powered models to an almost unbearable amount of derision. So, the more pretentious term 'spring motor mechanism' was substituted for clockwork by most of the railway model manufacturers. In the same way, some slight embarrassment was caused by the methods used in the manufacture of the new spring motor mechanized locomotives, which were mainly

104 Frank Roberts built this live steam model of the K 900; the prototype was introduced on New Zealand Railways in 1932.

126

composed of pieces of stout tinplate, soldered together. 'Planished steel plate' looked better than tinplate in catalogues and advertisements, so, once again, the gentle art of euphemism was practised, to everyone's advantage. The engines, however they were described, would usually run, after a single winding, for about 100 feet in Gauge O, and for half as long again in Gauge 1.

There are, today, many clockwork enthusiasts who collect these old trains, and some who get much pleasure from seeing them run. Operators of old clockwork locomotives have, however, many difficulties to overcome – the most obvious ones being the liability of springs to break, and the impossibility of obtaining replacements. And there are other – in human beings, they would probably be called temperamental – shortcomings with which lovers of clockwork trains have to contend. Changes of temperature, for example, are liable to affect the performance of spring-driven locomotives. Cold will contract a spring and make its metal more brittle, as well as thickening the oil that is so necessary for lubrication. Excessive heat may distort a spring, and, by thinning the oil, may affect the functioning of axles, bearings, and other mechanical parts. More, the general oiliness of clockwork motors makes them exceptionally liable to pick up dust and fluff. These, too, can easily collect on the usually oily wheels, reducing even further the limited hauling power of the engine and its range.

In spite of all its drawbacks, clockwork, as a means of motivating model trains, was never seriously challenged by an alternative method developed at roughly the same time. In the more limited friction locomotives and trolley cars, the power was supplied by

5 The model of the K 916 also ...lt by Frank Roberts is electric- ...y driven. This model covered 400 ...es during six months of an ...ibition.

heavy flywheels concealed inside the models. Each flywheel was
mounted on an axle, the ends of which were arranged to press down
heavily on the driving wheels. If a locomotive or car of this type
were pushed along the ground for some distance, sufficient
momentum would be stored up in the flywheel for the model,
when released, to keep running for a short distance under its own
power. The earliest toy friction locomotives were made largely of
wood.

The disappearance of steam locomotives from the real railways
of the world, described in Chapter 6, has caused many heart-aches
among modellers. But steam, as a source of motive power, had a
good run in its time – steam locomotives were part of the international scene for much longer than the stage coaches they
replaced, and they are now as universally accepted as symbols of
romance and elegance as the tall-masted sailing traders that have
virtually disappeared from the world's seas. Inevitably, then, the
model steam locomotive arouses strong feelings of admiration and
even, sometimes, of love. To the dedicated live steam addict, all
other forms of motive power are unworthy of serious consideration.

From the earliest days of model steam locomotives, many
problems had to be solved before any miniature engine could be
made to run successfully. These difficulties have aroused pro-
tective, even maternal, instincts in the engines' sponsors. Even the
rudimentary model steam locomotives of the pre-Bassett-Lowke
era – those known so fittingly as dribblers – behaved like awkward
babies. As they moved off, hissing and spitting, around their
strictly limited tracks, they could be relied on to leave large,
inconvenient pools of water in their wake. (If they were given
sufficient water, they would inevitably 'boil over' as soon as they
started to make steam. If they were not given sufficient water, the
boiler would be burned out. It was as simple as that.) But most
later model steam locomotives behave well if they are properly
cherished and fussed over – again, so like small children. They
have to be given water that is soft and clean; their source of heat
has to be exactly right; and – their most easily overlooked need of
all – they have to be kept constantly supplied with plenty of rich,
syrupy oil. If a model steam locomotive is properly provided with
all these things it is likely to work happily for years – for at least as
long as any engine powered by rival methods and probably longer.

The early commercial steam locomotives made by Märklin,
Bing and other German firms were, like the early clockwork
models, picturesque but not closely related to any known prototype. Those made in the United States – by Eugene Beggs, of
Paterson, New Jersey, the Weeden Manufacturing Company, of
New Bedford, Massachusetts, and other firms – were no more
closely geared to reality.

*Above, a 1 in. scale 5 in. gauge
live steam model of a 2–2–2
London and North-Western
Railway locomotive. The model,
now in the possession of his eldes
son, was built by A. D. Pole ove
a period of four years.*

*Below, one of the many models
running on the outdoor layout o
Swissminiatur near Lake Lugan
this is of the heavy freight electr
locomotive of Swiss Railways,
nicknamed 'The Crocodile'.*

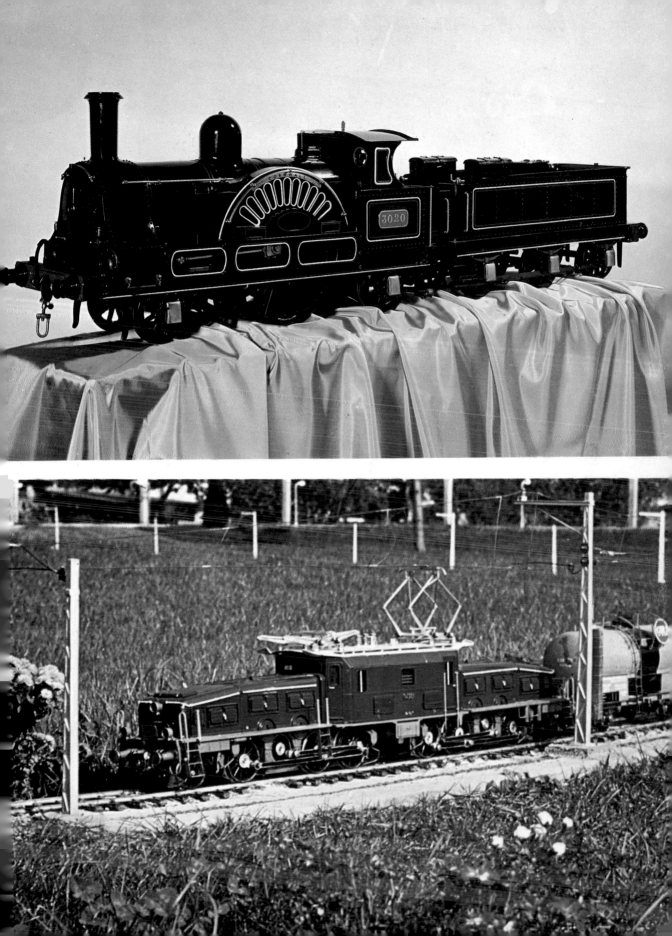

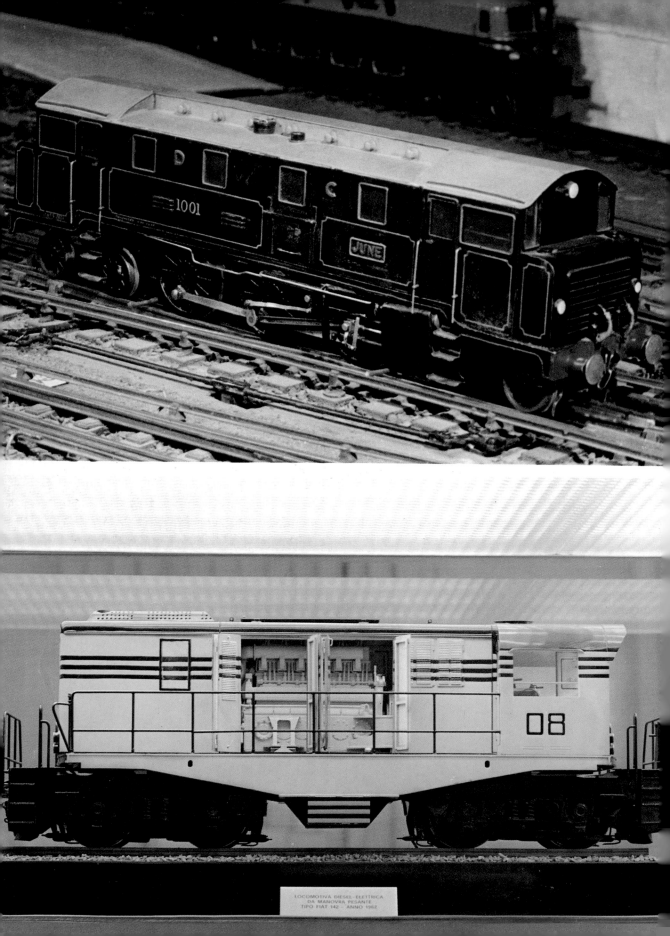

LOCOMOTIVA DIESEL-ELETTRICA
DA MANOVRA PESANTE
TIPO FIAT 142 - ANNO 1962

Even the colours of these early live steam models were chosen arbitrarily. Märklin sold black engines with scarlet wheels. Carette and Karl Bub's wares were printed in rich shades of green. In some countries, such as Sweden and the United States, the engines chosen to act (in the most approximate way) as prototypes had boiler covers made from polished Russia iron. Steam-powered models made to represent these usually looked in better shape after they had been running for a little time than did replicas of engines with painted boilers. All too often, the carefully painted surfaces of the latter would be blistered and blackened before steam had even been raised for a maiden journey. Märklin fitted wooden covers on the handrails of two of its live steam models so that these could be more easily handled when the boilers were hot.

It would be interesting to know how much of the fascination of model steam locomotives can be attributed to the ever-present element of danger that has led so many careful mothers to insist 'This train is not to be run unless father is in charge,' and has induced manufacturers such as Jehu Garlick, of Paterson, New Jersey, to claim in their advertisements 'This is just the thing to buy for your boys if they have the least desire for Steam Toys, it is really practical, perfectly safe, and impossible to explode.' Actually the chances of disaster have usually been grossly exaggerated. If the boiler has been properly sweated up, with pipes fitting snugly into accurately prepared holes, and if it has been fitted with a reliable safety valve, nothing serious is likely to happen. Normally, the valve will be set at a blow-off pressure of around 50 pounds to the square inch, which gives a reassuring factor of safety. In law, a sane man is usually assumed to intend the probable consequences of his actions. Daring operators of steam-driven models who deliberately screw down their models' safety valves for the sake of obtaining higher steam pressures must suffer patiently (like the drivers of the prototypes) the possible results of their own temerity.

In 1910, Wenman Bassett-Lowke introduced into his lists a splendid Gauge O steam model of the London and North Western Railway locomotive *Black Prince*. The magazine *Model Engineer* commented:

This engine is well made and the working arrangements are good. The wickless spirit lamp and oil-feed reservoirs are excellent ideas. The steam pipes are carried above the lamp so that they are exposed to the heat from the flames. This is a commendable arrangement, tending to dry the steam on its way to the cylinders. We consider the trial of the engine quite satisfactory. A working pressure of steam was obtained in less than ten minutes from lighting up, the boiler being filled three-quarters full with cold water at starting.

Above, a free lance model diesel locomotive made by Major Sparks 1930, now in the Muséon di ...do.

Below, a museum model of a diesel-electric shunting locomotive (switcher) of the Fiat type 142.

106 Above – A 3½ in. gauge chassis for an o–6–o engine having a 30 c.c. twin cylinder overhead valve water cooled petrol engine.

107 Left – The first 3 in. scale 4–6– Pacific type locomotive ever built.

108 Right, above – A live steam freight train made by Frank Robert The train is hauled by a model of the largest tank locomotive in use by New Zealand Railways.

109 Right, centre – The King Arthur of Southern Railways, modelled by E. F. Stratton in 5 in. gauge. The copper boiler has a work ing pressure of 100 pounds per square inch.

110 Right – An electrically driven model of the Beyer–Peacock– Garrat 4–6–4 + 4–6–4 locomotive made to a ¾ in. scale.

But Bassett-Lowke was in danger of dropping behind the times. The pace of life was quickening, and fewer and fewer people would be willing to wait for nine minutes for an engine to raise enough steam for a four minute journey. Electricity – instant, miraculous electricity – was elbowing steam off the stage.

The first electrically operated model locomotives may have been manufactured as early as 1850, for one was illustrated in the catalogue issued by Palmer and Hall, of Boston, Massachusetts, in that year. By 1884, the Novelty Electric Company of Philadelphia had certainly managed to produce and market a limited number of electric trains, but these were almost prohibitively expensive.

The first toy railways worked by electricity that were cheap enough to be successful commercial propositions were those brought out by Märklin Brothers in 1900. These models were designed to represent, very roughly, steam-driven prototypes – there were, at that time, no full-size electrically driven locomotives in regular use. The models were made to run on Gauge 1 track, and playing with them was a distinctly chancy business. They could be worked off low-tension current from an accumulator, which was rarely satisfactory because the current supply was all too liable to fail as soon as spectators arrived to view the novelty. Alternatively, they could be connected to the lighting mains, the

111 A finely-detailed electrically driven model made by Trix in Gauge HO of an 0–6–0 locomotive used in Prussia from 1883 to 1907. It was designed for either the 3-rail or 2-rail system.

current being carried through a simple carbon filament lamp resistance intended to control the train's speed. As soon as the engine was taken off the rails, the full 110 or 220 volts supply remained in the track. This made the new playthings quite unsuitable for use by children.

Then Märklins attempted to increase the appeal of their electrically operated models by bringing out resistances in small, closed casings. These cost nearly four times as much as the ugly old lamp resistances, but the problems of power supply were still not finally solved. One of the main difficulties to be overcome was that presented by the central third rail, which had to be insulated with rubber or fibre washers. Short circuits, which resulted when these washers were faulty, or when the long out-of-scale coupling links were allowed to hang down between the component parts of a train, were frequent occurrences.

Today, the problems of power supply have been largely ironed out, thanks to the pioneer work of such great firms as Märklin, which introduced in 1926 the 20 volt system, and Bassett-Lowke, which brought out late in 1932 a 20 volt alternating current motor in Gauge O with a reasonably priced transformer and resistor. These made it possible for a model train to be run off the house mains without difficulty or danger. Since then, a number of systems have been devised that will make small electric motors run satisfactorily and allow full control of speed and direction.

Before it can do its intended work, an electric circuit must have a properly arranged flow and return. There must be an insulated, current-carrying conductor that makes a path from the power unit, through the electric motor that drives the locomotive, and back to the source. If the circuit is broken – as, for example, by a switch – the work done by the engine is interrupted. Even the most sophisticated systems now in use are based upon this simple principle.

Most model railways today are run off a supply with a fairly low voltage – 12 volts is the most common. This is provided in one of four ways. Dry batteries may be used for very small and simple layouts, but this is an expensive method, and barely satisfactory, owing to the short life of a dry battery. Twelve volt accumulators are more often used, but they have one great drawback – they need re-charging periodically. Motor generators are inclined to be noisy and expensive. The most popular – and simplest – power source is a unit that works off the alternating current mains. This takes in electricity and lowers it to the safe level of 12 volts (or 16, or 24), transforming it at the same time from alternating to direct current. (This is done so that the supply, at the smaller voltage, shall be smooth and regular.) Most power units today incorporate controllers – devices which by varying the resistance can raise and

112 A Fleischmann model electric
locomotive with pantographs that
pick up current from an overhead
catenary just as the prototype does

113 A model of 'The Edelweiss
Local', a rack-and-pinion (cog-
wheel) electric locomotive used in
mountainous districts. Both model
and prototype are capable of
climbing spectacular grades.

lower the voltage between 0 and 12, 16 or 24 volts, making the trains move slowly or quickly as the operator chooses.

There are several ways in which current can be supplied to a moving model locomotive. One of the most straightforward is the two rail system. In this, the current is fed through one rail and set of wheels to the motor, returning to the source to complete the circuit by way of the opposite wheels and the rail on the other side of the track. This system appeals to those who attach particular importance to the exactly realistic appearance of their layouts, and, in spite of the relatively large amount of care that has to be taken if complete insulation is to be preserved, the two rail system is now the most often used in all scales smaller than O.

In other systems, the current may be carried through both running rails jointly, the circuit being completed by a third (conductor) rail, by an overhead wire or rail, or by a method known usually as stud contact, in which a series of inconspicuous metal pins or buttons set in the sleepers takes the place of the third rail. Where overhead contact wires are provided, it is possible to run two locomotives quite independently of one another over the same length of track – one uses surface contact, the other uses the overhead supply.

One of the greatest advantages of the electrification of model railways is the ease with which trains can now be controlled from a distance. The field-wound electric motors found in earlier models would always run in the same direction, irrespective of the direction of the current supplied. Reversing had to be carried out by complicated switching systems, operated, usually, by hand. The motor in general use today is the permanent magnet motor. To move in reverse a locomotive fitted with one of these engines, one has simply to reverse the direction of the power supply. This can be done, at a modern proprietary remote control panel, by the movement of a finger.

Electrification has no real disadvantages – except, possibly, that it renders even the best-equipped layout liable to occasional visits from the 'gremlins'. These are the mythical beasts, known to all modern railway modellers, that cause sudden, unexpected, and completely illogical failures. Breakdowns always seem to occur in the presence of distinguished visitors, and they last, usually, in spite of the most energetic efforts that can be made to get things going again, until the visitors, discouraged, have left. Then, as Henri Girod-Eymery, master mind of the Muséon di Rodo at Uzès, has pointed out, 'a mere patting on the baseboard is sufficient to induce the gremlins to energize the whole system again.' The management of full scale trade unions, M Girod-Eymery considers, is child's play compared to handling unpredictable gremlin teams.

9 Coaches and Freight Cars

The first passenger railway coach ever built was ordered by Robert Stephenson for the Stockton and Darlington line. It was designed to be drawn by a horse along the new railway. It had room for six passengers inside, with seats for fifteen more in exposed positions. It was, virtually, a road coach with a few minor adaptations. To make it reversible, there were shafts for a horse at each end.

The coaches made for the Liverpool and Manchester Railway also bore a strong resemblance to horse-drawn road coaches. This is easy to understand, for the men who designed them turned for reference to the only public vehicles they knew. In the Liverpool and Manchester coaches, though, a little more thought had been given to the powers of endurance of the passengers - the directors of the railway company had decided that all ticket-holders should be allowed to travel inside. On top of the coaches, there were racks in which the passengers' luggage travelled – literally – at the mercy of the elements.

The interiors of these early passenger coaches were starkly uncomfortable. Rather than submit to the torments of long journeys spent on hard, straight-backed seats, members of the richer classes usually elected to travel instead in their own personal carriages. These were mounted on flat trucks which were coupled to the rear of the public trains. On one occasion, an elderly gentleman who had insisted on being taken from London to Brighton in his own conveyance, although he had been warned of the possible consequences, was left stranded in one of the longer tunnels on the way down, when a coupling broke. He shouted unheard as the train to which he had been attached disappeared in the distance, and when an engine that had been sent to rescue him approached, belching out flames and sparks through the darkness, he must have thought that his last moment had come. The wealthy did not give up their privileged manner of travel, in spite of these occasional small misadventures, until the standards of comfort of the railway companies' first class coaches had changed noticeably for the better.

No one, however pampered, could have grumbled at the luxurious conditions in which the more favoured passengers were able to travel by the end of the nineteenth century. The coaches

14 A scene on the Midland Railway exhibit in the Derby Municipal Museum showing an assortment of goods wagons (freight cars) of the period about 1900.

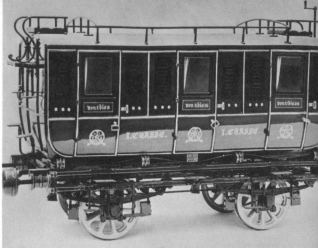

115 Above, left – A model of the second class coach Hannibal used on the first horsedrawn railway line in central Europe which was built between 1825 and 1832.

116 Above, right – A model of a first class coach used on the Munich–Augsburg railway in 1841.

117 Below, left – The prototype of this second and first class coach was built in 1858.

118 Below, right – 1906 was the year the prototype of this model second and third class coach was introduced in Germany.

119 Right, above – A France–Train model of a first and second class coach once used by French National Railway. The observation box is seen on the left.

120 Right, centre above – A Lilliput model of the Wagon Lits coach used during the signing of the Armistice of World War 1.

121 Right, centre below – A 3½ in. gauge model of a London North Eastern Railway first class corridor coach. It has internally fitted electric lights.

122 Right, bottom – Great Western Railway all-wood model coaches of the 'clerestory' type made by Jim Whittaker for his 16.5 mm. layout. All first class on the left and third class/brake on the right.

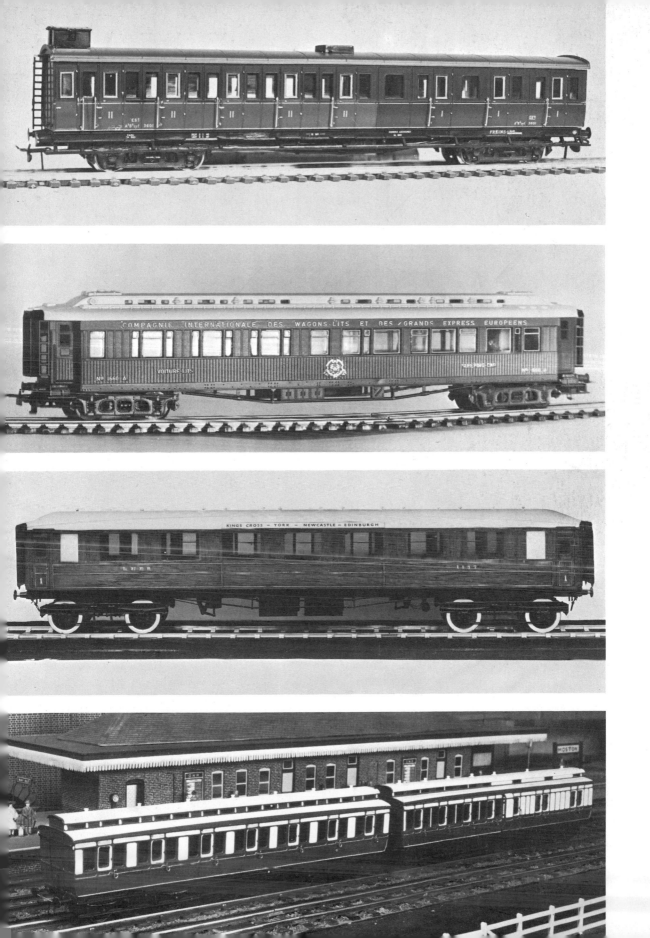

made specially for the reigning sovereigns of the civilized world were like miniature palaces, with comfortable lounges fitted with sumptuous furniture, beautifully appointed bathrooms, tactfully secluded toilets, and facilities for wining and dining that were as lavish and tasteful as those to which the principal passengers were used in their numerous and exemplary homes.

As most railway modellers are liable to spend more time in the coaches than they are on the foot-plates of locomotives, however much they may romantically imagine the opposite to be the case, they tend to be particularly conscious of the authenticity, or otherwise, of these important elements of a model railway system.

In the bad old days before the present techniques of plastic injection moulding were developed, modellers had to choose between three alternative methods of providing themselves with miniature coaching stock – they could have hand-made models, models made of tinplate with tinprinted exteriors, or wooden models to which were applied paper skins, lithoprinted with panelling shadows, livery lines, and other surface markings.

Hand-made model railway coaches are still very much with us, and are not likely to disappear completely from the model engineering scene, since some of the finest craftsmen in the world regard the difficulties presented by their construction as a considerable challenge. However, even the most bigoted scratch-builders are often prepared to save themselves unprofitable labour by drawing at least partly on the resources of the modern world. The provision of smooth-running, true-to-prototype bogies and bolsters for a rake of model coaches must necessarily involve a lot of repetition work, and many craftsmen buy these as ready-made castings or mouldings from the commercial firms that specialize in their production.

There are several different methods by which model coach bodies may be hand-constructed on commercially-built underframes. Some modellers use thin, resin-bonded plywood for the sides of their coaches, cutting out the windows by hand, a task that demands endless patience and precision. Others use nickel silver or brass, punching out the windows (for the sake of speed) with specially made dies. Modellers who would find these techniques difficult will usually make their coach bodies from one of the new, easily cut materials such as styrene sheet, or they may use laminated sheeting made by gluing or pasting together pieces of stout paper or thin card. (Japanese modellers are especially fond of using paper as their raw material.) Even the unhandy may experience in in a limited way the joys of creation, since there are on the market many excellent and easily assembled coach kits in which the main parts are made from pre-formed styrene sheet.

Model coaches made of tinplate to the coarsest of coarse scales

died out with the disappearance of the old 'anything goes' standards that were good enough for most pre-Second World War nurseries and playrooms. Under competitive conditions that keep prices within the ordinary collector's reach, coaches are now marketed with plastic-framed windows, exactly to scale, concertina connections that are really convincing, sliding doors, realistic interior fittings, and lighting systems that have a constant intensity whatever the motion of the train. Rivarossi, the Italian company, even offers a four-wheel baggage car that has a whistle incorporated. The whistle is operated by a 1.5 volt torch battery, and is actuated only when the car passes over a special section of track.

The lighting of the interiors of model railway coaches by high frequency current is a sphere of activity that appeals to some really expert modellers, since the effects produced when a tiny, illuminated train is operated in darkness or near-darkness are often most impressive. At the Pendon Museum of Miniature Landscape and Transport, in Long Wittenham, Berkshire, England, in one of the most ingenious model railway systems in operation today, the track

127 Top – A Märklin model of a beer car.

128 Below – A Siemens 30 MV transformer model from Trix is loaded on the Fleischmann 16-wheel low-loader of the German Federal Railways.

*9 Top – A Marklin model of a
mical container car in Bayer
ery.*

*Below – An automatic centre-
charging high-sided wagon of
rman Federal Railways
delled by Lilliput.*

is fed with the normal direct current supply of 12 volts. At the same
time, it is fed with a supply of 10 volts at approximately 50 kilo-
cycles. (That is, one thousand times the frequency of the ordinary
alternating current mains.) At this frequency, the current can pass
quite easily through a small condenser. This condenser blocks the
direct current from passing through the tiny 'grain of wheat' lamp
mounted at the centre of each coach, while the induction of the
motor itself is sufficient to keep the alternating current out of the
traction circuit. The light is distributed to each of the compartments
in a coach, from the central lamp, by means of a length of transparent
plastic bar. This has a tiny prismatic facet cut into it wherever there
would be a lamp in the prototype coach.

Most prototype railways carry freight cars as well as passenger
coaches – on some lines, indeed, the former may be found to
provide the greater part of the operating company's turnover.
Craftsmen who make their own model freight cars (and collectors
who buy them) are usually found to have a distinct preference for
cars of the older types that are rapidly vanishing, or for the stream-

lined, easily handled vehicles of the present and future. To appreciate the difference, one must know how the whole business of
the carriage of freight by rail has recently been rationalized in
certain countries.

For several decades, the mixed goods train was a familiar sight
in many railway systems. A train of this kind would meander at a
leisurely pace across the countryside, picking up a freight wagon
or two here, setting down one or two there, and working, when the
lines it was to use were not needed for faster trains, to a casually
compiled timetable. The incessant shunting and re-marshalling to
which these old goods trains were subject produced arrangements
of wagons of all kinds that were endlessly fascinating to those who
appreciated the commercial and industrial scene. Fish wagons
would be followed by gunpowder containers; refrigerated cars
would be coupled to timber trucks; gravel hoppers would rumble
up the tracks next to horse boxes; snow ploughs might be found in
close proximity to banana vans, or wine tankers. A train marshalled
for a single journey might contain as many as a hundred different
vehicles, each designed and decorated individually to conform to
its owner's particular wishes.

Modern freight trains are organized more efficiently and economically. Today, in most systems, freight loads are carried at
high speeds between important centres, and operate to exact
schedules. The flat wagons used in these new freight trains are
usually kept coupled semi-permanently in sets, like the coaches
in the multiple unit passenger trains. Loaded containers are
brought to the freight terminals by road, and are there transferred
to the flat railway trucks. The great difference between the old
method of operating freight trains and the new has produced a
corresponding difference between the various components that
make up the two kinds of train.

The enormous range of freight cars of the older sort provided
almost unlimited scope for railway model manufacturers who
wanted to stimulate demand for their wares, a ceaseless succession
of new lines. Using lithography – that is (in this context) the
technique of colour printing on sheet metal – the great firms of
Bing, Ives, American Flyer and their competitors produced and
marketed ranges of model freight wagons as various as those seen
on any prototype railway, even the busiest. Collectors now pay
high prices for early examples of these firms' classified model cars
that are still in reasonably good conditio 1, and unrestored.

Careful as they were to tailor exactly a large proportion of their
models for the American market, even the directors of the great
firm of Bing were caught by surprise by the prohibition of alcoholic
beverages in the United States in 1930–34. Bing had been making
model beer cars in Gauge O and Gauge 1, with lithographed sides,

*Above, this museum model, part
cut away, shows the type of first
class carriage in use on the Liverpool and Manchester Railway fro
1830.*

*Below, a commercial model of a
three-container freight wagon no
in use on British Railways.*

for retail in America. When the advertisement of intoxicating liquors in that country was made illegal, Bing was forced to overprint each of the beer cars it intended to send over the Atlantic, obliterating with black rectangles the offending word beer, or even, in certain instances, the whole sentence in which it was contained. These cars, with their emendations, are now keenly sought for by collectors, their market value being increased as much by their curiosity as by their rarity.

Popular with all modellers who take an active interest in United States railroad practice are the the caboose cars that bring up the rear of each American freight train. Known familiarly as bedhouses, bouncers, doghouses, monkey wagons, (and by other less printable names), these cars act as travelling quarters for the trains' conductors, offices for paperwork, and as equipment stores for the crews.

The earliest cabooses were, simply, primitive boxcars with windows cut in the sides, and a few other less noticeable modifications. Later, when caboose cars were built specially for the purpose, further changes were made. The doors that had been found, previously, in the sides of the boxcars tended to be dangerous for the train crews to use, and they fell into disfavour. So, end platforms were added.

The most distinctive feature of a caboose – the cupola, or lookout cabin on the roof – is said to have been invented by a Chicago and North Western conductor about the year 1863. Allotted, while his own pride and joy went away for repair, a battered old boxcar with a gap in the roof, the indignant conductor stood on a pile of freight boxes and put his head and shoulders through the hole. As he waved flippantly to people beside the line, he realized that he had found a perfect vantage point, from which he could view without effort the whole of the train and the track on which it was running. Accordingly, he asked one of the railroad company's accommodating carpenters to build for him, on that old car, a glazed shelter, and, inside the car, a platform on which he could stand. Model caboose cars, with cupolas of the standard box-like type, or with the variations introduced in recent decades, are made and marketed now by Märklin, Rivarossi, LIMA, Fleischmann, and the other principal European manufacturers, as well as by American firms working for their home market.

Another type of model railway freight car that appeals to certain collectors is the circus wagon. Circuses have a romantic glamour that many people – old as well as young – find irresistible. Long before the end of the nineteenth century, manufacturers of model railway equipment had started to turn this popular weakness to their own advantage and profit. Milton Bradley and Company's pull on-a-string wooden circus trains, marketed between 1880

lection of commercially made
ng stock.

149

and 1890, competed with those made by the Bliss Manufacturing Company on which were emblazoned BARNUM'S GREAT RAILROAD CIRCUS, GREAT MORAL SHOW AND MENAGERIE and other tempting legends.

Ives followed, in the 1890's, with a cast iron model circus train that incorporated an elephant car. Thirty years or so later, this firm brought out an elaborate model railway circus set, which included a locomotive and tender, a cloth circus tent with cars on which it could be carried, brightly painted cages with animals, and enough booths and sideshows to furnish an exciting funfair background. Märklin and Hoge have also marketed model circus trains that collectors find attractive. Until recently, Triang-Hornby offered an operating giraffe car. Whenever this car, with its protruding load, approached an overhead obstacle, a magnetic device came into operation, causing the long-necked animal carried in the car to duck its head. 'Unlikely,' said the Triang-Hornby catalogue of the firm's skilfully contrived phenomenon, 'and extremely amusing!'

131 Top – Lima have modelled t... French wagon used for transport... melted iron.

132 Below – A model of an Italia... auto-transporter modelled by Rivarossi.

Top – A model of an American log car made by Tyco.

Below – A Trix model of a used for transporting cement.

Novelties as ingenious as that (if not necessarily so humorous) are being offered at the present time by all the world's great manufacturers of railway models. It would be impossible to review here even a small percentage of the superbly detailed commercially produced freight cars that can be bought for a domestic layout for quite a small outlay. Even a young collector with fairly limited means could acquire from Märklin (as this book is being compiled) a low-sided eight wheel freight car loaded with two trucks; an eight wheel pressurized gas wagon of the type used by the VTG (Vereiningte Tanklager und Transportmittel GmbH) concern; a crane truck with a slewing crane with a movable jib and jib support. Or from Rivarossi he could get an Italian flat type car loaded with an Honest John missile; a flat car on trucks carrying a Sherman tank; or one of the huge articulated cars used in enormous convoys for exporting new automobiles from Italy to foreign markets. And all the most enterprising companies add new lines to their lists every year. The collector of model freight cars has (literally) never before had it so good.

10 Layouts

Small-scale locomotives and miniature replicas of coaches and other rolling stock are often shown against plain backgrounds, and may give much pleasure when viewed in this way. To some owners however, there is no more appropriate and satisfying setting for their models than a layout – and the more accurately detailed and carefully finished the layout is, the more they approve.

The frame of mind in which a railway modeller first decides to make a new layout is not unlike that of a traveller who proposes to set out on a long journey.

From the start, he has to realize that by merely embarking on the project, he is inevitably committing himself to weeks, months, or even years of hard labour. (One of the most admired modellers in the world began his current layout in 1937 – that is, two years before the start of the Second World War – and is still hoping to complete it 'some day'.)

He is inevitably committing himself, too, to some disturbance of his regular domestic routines. If he is tactful, he will take steps to appease anyone that his plans can possibly inconvenience – even, in extreme circumstances, his wife. One of the most considerable items on his expenses sheets may well be the boxes of chocolates, or other gifts, that he has to produce, like olive branches, at critical moments in his domestic history.

Then, the man who has decided to make a layout has to ask himself if he wants to work on his own, or with members of his family, or with friends. Many hands make light work, but while some railway modellers enjoy working in company, other find it difficult to co-operate. The most successful partnerships seem to be those in which a modeller who most enjoys (say) building locomotives or rolling stock is ready to join forces with one who prefers to specialize in miniature track-laying, or the construction of small-scale landscapes.

At an early stage, the layout maker has to decide on the form that his system is to take. As this decision may be almost irrevocable, he has to consider very carefully the possible alternatives.

First, he has to take a long hard look at the space available. If he can afford to allot a whole large room or even an entire building

35 An exhibition layout using Arnold equipment.

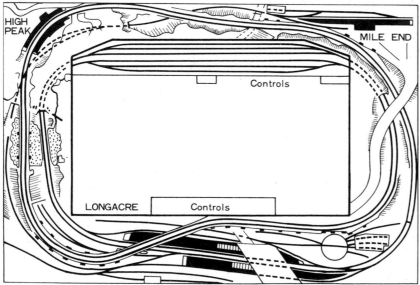

136 *Above – Two viaducts on part of Ross Pochin's layout which is modelled in 4 mm. scale and 18 mm. gauge.*

137 *Left – An example of a good layout built in Gauge TT by the Macclesfield Model Railway Group, showing the central area left clear for ease of operation.*

138 *Right – These simple layouts can be bought as packs and are especially suitable for beginners.*

to the project he has in mind he can plan his layout on an ambitious and exciting scale, but modellers as fortunate as this are few. Most have to confine their activities to a part of a room – a corner of one, possibly – or part of an attic or garage. This need not necessarily be the disadvantage that it sounds. Some of the world's most splendid layouts have been made in a limited space.

At this stage, the modeller will probably decide to draw out some tentative track plans, as the boundaries in which his layout is to be contained will inevitably affect the way in which the tracks will run. If he is the sort of person who likes to daydream, to build castles in the air, he will find the time he spends in this theoretical activity peculiarly satisfying. Many books have been written and published about this one aspect of railway modelling alone, and it is certain that only a very small proportion of the thousands and thousands of layouts that are planned, and drawn out are, later, actually translated into reality.

Although, in practice, track plans are often sketched out roughly on the backs of bus tickets, cigarette packets, or other unsuitable surfaces, they should, ideally, be drawn out carefully and to scale. Many rooms used to house model railway layouts contain architectural features such as chimney breasts and permanently built-in cupboards that cannot be easily altered. These have to be accurately plotted on the track plans if they are likely to be in the way of any proposed lines. Doorways and windows, too, must not be forgotten if a model railway layout is to be fitted happily into normal household surroundings. Parts of a layout can be made so that they are easily removable – a section of baseboard can be fitted with hinges, for instance, so that a family right-of-way can be restored whenever it is needed – but if no special precautions are taken the disaster rate may tend to go up on any layout that contains one of these easily overlooked hazards. A model locomotive that has taken a sudden nose-dive to the floor is not likely to be any better for its fall.

Even a comparatively simple layout – such as a plain circle of track – needs careful consideration. Layouts have a strange tendency to become more complicated as modelling proceeds – branch lines, loop lines, stations, sidings, and other features are added as the modeller's inventiveness becomes increasingly active. If the original track has been placed too near the outer boundary of the space available – that is, too near the edge of a table or baseboard – it may not be possible for any of these extensions to be made, or not as many as the modeller would like. The most successful layout-makers, then, are those who look ahead.

It often happens that a beginner starts with a circular or oval layout and then finds that there are limits to the fascination of a continuous run (trains going round and round one of these endless tracks do have a disquieting similarity to small animals chasing their own tails). At this stage, the advantages of a layout built on the point-to-point system usually become apparent. At least, in a layout designed according to this plan, the trains do appear to be leaving one place and going to another. An alternative type of layout favoured by many modellers is the return loop – the name, by itself, suggesting the out, around a loop and back conformation that makes this kind of layout so easy to operate, and so satisfying. Other modellers devise layouts that allow both point-to-point and continuous working. They find that combined layouts of this kind are liable to please both the expert operator and the interested but untechnical visitor.

One of the most striking developments in layout design in recent years has been the increase in popularity of the L-shaped terminus layout. This is a layout planned within a right angle on the terminus-to-terminus principle. It has great space-saving qualities that make it especially valuable for adoption in normal domestic circumstances, since it can be arranged within conveniently narrow boundaries – as, for example, on shelves – and set against only two adjoining walls of a room.

For trains to be operated successfully on a layout of this kind, a fiddle yard usually has to be incorporated – an arrangement of sidings, that is, where locomotives, carriages and wagons can be marshalled, or allowed to rest when not needed for the main lines, and from which stock can be lifted by hand for overhaul, cleaning or repair.

On some layouts, the fiddle yard is hidden behind buildings or specially arranged landscape features. This happens, as a rule, when those who have designed the layout believe that maintenance and similar operations should be carried out where spectators cannot see. Other people prefer to keep all the workings of their lines, even the most functional, in full view. In layouts designed specially for use in public exhibitions, it is usually found advantageous to have a comparatively large proportion of the track screened from the eyes of inquisitive visitors. This has an interesting psychological side-effect. There seems to be a great fascination, to the lay mind, in the sight of a train disappearing into a tunnel, and even more in the sight of a train reappearing from one. If, owing to some concealed re-marshalling, the train that emerges is not the train that disappeared, an element of magic is introduced that never fails to delight the uninitiated.

When he has decided on his track plan, and on the disposition of the concealed areas of his layout, if any, the modeller has next to arrange for his track to be raised to a convenient level. A layout *can* be set down on the floor, but one assembled in this lowly way will have many disadvantages – it will be difficult to build and

Above, Bill Knap of New Zealand layout. The illustration shows the dock area.

Below, part of the St. Gotthard Railway layout in the Swiss Transport Museum. The whole system was built to a scale of 1 to 90.

Overleaf, the station and town area on a Gauge N Arnold Rapido layout.

to operate, it will be liable to be trodden on, and it will act as a trap for dust and dirt. The last drawback should be enough to disqualify it, for no layout that is to accomodate moving mechanical models can provide satisfactory running conditions for them unless it can be kept satisfactorily clean.

Layouts in the smaller scales, such as TT and N, can normally be raised, by being set out on suitable tables, to levels at which they are easily manageable. If a table so used is likely to be needed for any other purposes before the layout is scrapped, the track can be laid on top of a removable sheet of chipwood or hardboard.

Layouts in the medium and larger scales are usually set out on baseboards supported by specially made timber structures. It is essential that the baseboards should be absolutely flat and level and that they remain so, since track will always tend to conform to the contours of the surface on which it is laid. Flimsy materials such as cardboard are worse than useless; materials such as tongued and grooved wooden boards that expand and contract with changes of temperature and humidity are as bad because their movement is disastrous to trackwork; plywood, even in the more substantial thicknesses, is rejected by many modellers on account of its liability to warp; hardboard, which is cheap and comparatively inert, is generally preferred, though it tends to be noisy, is difficult to drive pins into, and needs support from rigid cross-bearers at fairly frequent intervals.

The best baseboard material of all is probably chipboard – factory made, from wood chips bonded with resin. This sheeting is strong enough to need very little support, has little tendency to warp, and is soft enough to take with comparative ease the small pins used for fixing track. If a layout is not to be absolutely immovable – and making the whole sub-structure portable is always a sensible precaution, even if there is no immediate intention of carrying the layout round to exhibitions, since few people or societies can be really sure that they will never have to move their home – the baseboards must be of a reasonable size for handling. In any case, one should never have to lean too far over a baseboard because the track and models on it are bound to suffer.

When his supporting surfaces are ready, the modeller can start to build up the main forms of his landscape – he will certainly want to do this, using the techniques described in Chapter 14, if his railway is not to appear to run across monotonously flat ground. He can buy or make and lay his track, too, if indeed he has not begun to do so already. He cannot go much further than this without pausing to decide how exactly truthful his layout is going to be.

What, in this or any other context, is truth? Philosophers and other wise men have debated that question for many centuries

above, the city of Port in John Allen's Gauge HO layout – 'The Gorre and Daphetid Railroad'.

below, the Gauge O layout run the Romney, Hythe and Dymchurch Light Railway.

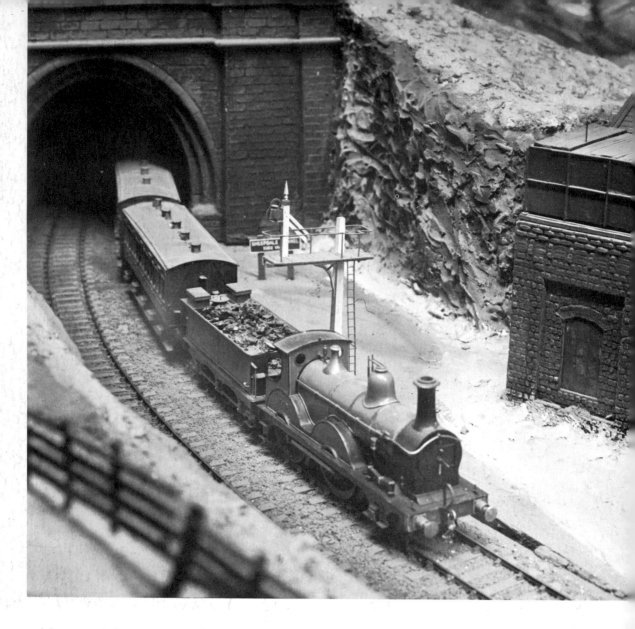

without arriving at any definition that is much more satisfactory than 'Truth is the intellectual apperception of objective reality.' There are certain railway modellers, however, who believe that truth is readily demonstrable without recourse to lengthy dialectics. They prove their point, or try to, by the perfection of their layouts. In order to appreciate the exacting standards worked to by the railway modeller who is fanatically concerned with truth, the less assured may care to study how one of these perfectionists will plan and carry out his display.

From the start, the man aiming at absolute truth will resolutely turn his back on the vague, the guessed at and the generalized.

On many layouts, notably those seen in the more public museums, locomotives, passenger coaches and freight cars drawn from several

139 Above – A very realistic scene on the Midland Railway Gauge O layout in the Derby Municipal Museum.

140 Above, right – A view of the Lone Pine Yard on Whitney K. Towers' Alturas and Lone Pine layout.

141 Right – A simple method of constructing baseboard supports.

different areas and from various periods of history will be put together, regardless of the fact that the prototypes may have been separated in geographical terms by hundreds of miles, and in time span by tens of years. Each individual model on a layout of this sort may be an accurate replica of an original, but the layout itself will not represent any particular place, nor will it be typical of any particular time, since it will not have been designed to fulfil either of these aims. A layout of this kind may have a wide appeal, for the operator can run on it almost any model he fancies, but it will not satisfy the perfectionist.

The perfectionist's layout will be invariably the fulfilment of a dream. He will have set out deliberately to re-create in solid, three-dimensional form his vision of the one small part of the world's

surface that means more to him than any other, seen in a single instant in time.

He may not even know why he has condemned himself so irrationally to this exacting labour – the feeling is as inexplicable and as compulsive as falling in love (and is apt to last a good deal longer!). He may have some happy memories in the deeper layers of his subconscious of one particular line or station he has known in childhood; he may want to reproduce exactly some obscure line that has previously escaped the attention of all modellers; or – if he tends to look ahead, rather than back – his imagination may be fired by some new, exciting development in railway technology.

Once he has taken the great decision about the standards of truth to which he is going to work, the perfectionist is committed

142 A view of the depòt at the Anatomopolis station in the Gur-Rug Gauge O layout in the Muséon di Rodo.

164

43 A layout begins to take shape.

to a programme of research so detailed and exhausting that a dis-interested observer could be forgiven for regarding it as crazy. In one layout recently brought into existence, for example, the freight trains are marshalled exactly as they would have been on a Thursday in July a little more than thirty years ago. Not as they would have been on a Wednesday or a Friday, it should be noticed, for on those days each of the freight trains that ran on the prototype line included a meat wagon. On Thursdays, a microscopic exam-ination of dusty records has revealed, the freight trains carried consignments of fish instead. If that is not the ultimate limit of virtuosity in railway modelling, what is?

Whatever the standards to which he decides to work, the maker of a layout – and all those assisting him in the enterprise – must

4 Left – A small part of a superb
layout constructed by David
Jenkinson in 4 mm. scale.

5 Above – The dock area at the
City of Port in John Allen's Gauge
O masterpiece, The Gorre and
Daphetid Railroad.

summon up enough energy and patience to keep going until the
project is finished, or until all interest has evaporated, whichever
is the sooner. Unlike most journeys, the construction of a model
railway layout can be abandoned at any stage, and there is no
particular virtue in reaching the end. The greatest satisfactions
come in the process of growth. A completed layout – that is, one
on which there is no longer any work left to be carried out – will
often seem as dull and as moribund as an aged patient in a geriatric
ward.

For this reason, it would be almost impossible to make a com-
prehensive catalogue of the best model railway layouts in the
world. Long before the catalogue was complete, many of the layouts
listed would have begun their slow but inevitable process of

deterioration. It is a sad experience, to visit a layout that has been described only recently in the most glowing terms, and to find that in the brief time that has elapsed since the description was written the layout has become somewhat jaded, slightly dusty, and full of the subtle but unmistakable symptoms that tell of neglect and decay. We know many outstanding layouts, therefore, only from photographs taken in the the happy period of time when they were at their peak of condition. The inclusion of a layout in the short survey that follows does not necessarily mean that it will be at its best, or even that it will exist at all, by the time these words are read.

Monterey, in California, has been described as the most glorious meeting of land and sea on earth. It is appropriate, then, that

146 Above – The loco yard, showing the engine shed and coaling stage in the Midland Railway layout at the Derby Municipal Museum.

147 Right – Two further views of the area around Anatomopolis station in the Gur-Rug layout.

there should be situated in Monterey a model railroad layout that many people believe is the most beautiful and spectacular in the whole world. It is known by the provocative name The Gorre and Daphetid (pronounced, Gory and Defeated). So much artistry and technical skill have gone into the construction of this miniature railroad that it has earned for its creator, John Allen, the title by which he has become universally known – The Wizard of Monterey.

John Allen began his great layout in 1954, and he is still building. It occupies an area of 425 square feet, with another 200 square feet of aisle space from which operation is carried out. Much of the magnificently detailed scenery that extends in places from floor to ceiling was built before tracklaying began so that the road-bed had to be graded in true prototypical manner before the hand-made track could be laid and ballasted.

Locomotives and rolling stock that run on the Gorre and Daphetid Railroad are realistically weathered so that they will appear hard worked by the mountainous line. The fireboxes in the locomotives cast a true-to-life fiery glow down on to the tracks as they battle up the gradients with their heavy freight cars. When a locomotive pauses over the ash pit to dump its cinders, a glowing cloud of smoke belches from the pit as the fireman does his job. That is just one of the many realistic operational scenes devised by John Allen for his layout, and he has worked so hard, and with so

148 Dave Moore's New Zealand $\frac{3}{16}$ in. scale layout incorporates a sawmill and beyond are two tunne

much ingenuity, that the little towns and industrial areas he has
created seem to be alive with activity.

Another ambitious American layout is the Pacific Beach and
Western, owned by the members of the Pacific Beach Model
Railroaders Club, Inc., and situated in a building on the San Diego
County Fairgrounds at Del Mar, California. There are over 2800
feet of Gauge HO track in the layout.

Again, many thousands of man-hours have been devoted to the
careful simulation of typical southwestern United States scenery.
A range of mountains, nearly fifty feet long, reaches almost to the
ceiling of the exhibition room. Operators, sitting at control panels
built into the top of this range can see almost the entire layout
from their lofty vantage point. There are just a few parts of the
system, though, that they cannot see from the appropriately
named Mountainair panels – an 11-track passenger yard and a 15-
track freight yard have actually been made *inside* the mountain.
These yards have been given names (can you guess?) North
Underhill and South Underhill.

There are many impressive realistic layouts to be seen in Great
Britain today. One of the most famous – the Gauge O Midland
Railway layout – is being carefully preserved in the County
Borough of Derby's Museum and Art Gallery. Derby's change of
status from a sleepy country market town to an important industrial

centre dates back to 1844, when the directors of the newly formed Midland Railway decided to make the place their headquarters. The commemorative layout shows in the finest detail the methods of operation practised by the Company in and about the year 1900 and is, in effect, an important repository of historical information.

One of the most notable developments in British railway modelling in recent years has been the growth of a wry, humorous element in what was previously regarded as the essentially serious business of layout-making. Typical of the new, mainly-for-laughter systems that are being featured more and more frequently in club and society exhibitions is the Far Twittering and Oysterperch Line, with its hilariously unpractical locomotives *Nellie*, *Hero*, *James* and *Wilbur*, which has been devised and shown widely to highly appreciative audiences by Eric Fox and Paul Towers, late Editor of the British railway modellers' magazine, *Model Railway News*. This noticeable drift towards high comedy may have resulted, to a certain extent, from the fantastic joke railways and other crazy-logic machines created since the Second World War by the successful British commercial artist Rowland Emett.

One of the most interesting model railway layouts in France today has, too, an underlying element of good humour, though the intentions of its present controller are rather more serious than those of the makers of the Far Twittering and Oysterperch Line. The French layout is known now as GUR-RUG. It is to be seen at the Museon di Rodo, at Uzès.

The GUR-RUG dates back to 1923. It was started, at that time, in England, by W. F. P. Kelly, who was a well-known model-maker. Mr Kelly had a pronounced whimsical streak in his nature, and as his original plans for the layout were intricate, and bore a striking likeness to the intestinal system of a higher mammal, it seemed quite appropriate that his model railway should be set in an imaginary country, that this imaginary country should be eventually dubbed Gutland, and that its imaginary capital city should be given the name Anatomopolis. As Kelly was equally fond of British and Continental European railways, Gutland was placed in an island position in the middle of the English Channel, from where it was (hypothetically) connected by tunnels to both England and France. This bit of freelance geography conveniently allowed locomotives and rolling stock of British, French, German and Swiss origin to have access to Gutland track, as well as the O Gauge, 7 millimetre (0.28 inch) scale models designed and made by the owner of the layout to the national (freelance) Gutland Railways specifications.

The Gutland layout had to be moved, for various reasons, two or three times during the lifetime of Kelly. Each time it underwent certain changes. It had just been re-located in a new house at

Hythe, in Kent, when Kelly died. In his last will and testament he gave his friend Geoffrey Percy Keen, President of the Model Railway Club of Great Britain, full right and power to dispose of the layout as Keen thought fit.

And that is how the Gutland railway happens, now, to be in France. Both Keen and Kelly had known, and liked, Henri Girod-Eymerey, the French model railway enthusiast, since 1931. Faced with the task of finding a new owner and custodian for his friend's layout, Keen asked M Girod-Eymerey to accept the bequest. M Girod-Eymerey agreed, and the layout was carefully dismantled, packed, and shipped over the English Channel in two large British Railways containers. In the move (or shortly after) it acquired its present name. At Uzès, it is known as the GUR-RUG, which is a combination of the phrases G.U.R. (Gutland Uzetian Railway) and R.U.G. (Réseau Uzétien de Gutland).

It would be unreasonable to expect a layout that has changed owners, and that has passed from one country to another, to retain its original identity in every respect – and railway modelling would be a sterile business if that could happen. As soon as a suitable closed gallery had been built at Uzès to accommodate the new acquisition, M Girod-Eymerey and his helpers started to acquire more rolling stock, and they are now able to mount one train for night travel, two daylight expresses, one international long distance express, one local passenger train, one push-and-pull suburban train, one mail train with a passenger coach, and various freight trains and special trains.

In Switzerland, one of the most satisfying layouts is on view at the Swiss Institute of Transport and Communications at Lucerne. This working model shows the northern ramp of the alpine Gotthard Line – between Erstfeld Station and the Naxberg Tunnel – and is carried out to a scale-ratio of 1 : 87 (Gauge HO). The layout includes 382 yards of track, 60 switches, 26 signals, and 18 different automatic block stations. Thirty traction vehicles and more than two hundred carriages and cars have been collected, so that it is possible for fourteen separate trains to be seen running at any one time.

The logging railroads of the United States are well known to most modellers, since they are so often used as prototypes. New Zealand has had some picturesque logging lines, too – known, there, as bush tramways, as they were constructed under the Tramways Act. Most of these lines were built between the years 1890 and 1930 to the standard New Zealand gauge of 3 feet 6 inches, and few were more than ten miles long. They were crude, but efficient – usually, the engines burned sawdust and waste wood, so that once the process had started, nothing was needed to keep things going, other than this fuel, except lubricating oil and labour.

The lines were not used just to convey logs from the bush to the mill – the saw-millers actually logged from the tramway. The tracks were laid right into the trees, and at the railhead a steam-powered winch or hauler was used to pull logs to the track from up to half a mile away. Then, the logs would be taken to the mill on the un-coupled log buggies. When the bush had been cleared from the neighbourhood of the line, the line would be moved to another area, and the whole operation would be repeated. Because of this, the trackwork was never up to main-line standards – it was always temporary, as was the sawmill itself. (It was cheaper to close down a mill and move it to a new site once a district had been cleared, than it was to transport logs many miles over rugged country.)

Today, the bush tramways have gone – they have been replaced by crawler tractors, trucks and electricity. But, one of the most splendid model railway layouts in New Zealand – the Taputerangi Timber Company's Bush Tramway, built by R. H. Stott – makes a valiant attempt to re-create the vanished era. This prominent member of the New Zealand Model Railway Guild has spent many holidays in the bush photographing and measuring relics, and interviewing veterans of the old saw-milling days. His layout may look a little slap-happy and dilapidated – but in that it is completely true to the prototype!

There could be no more efficiently superintended layout anywhere in the world than that made and operated by the members of the Melbourne Model Railway Society in Australia. Just to read the Book of Rules and Regulations issued by the committee would be a daunting experience for the timid. 'DO NOT HANDLE ANY LOCOMOTIVE – CLUB OR PRIVATE; THIS RULE MUST BE STRICTLY ADHERED TO' is Bye Law 2E; 'DO NOT place locos or rolling stock on the scenery at any time' is Bye Law 2L; and there are many others, equally firm, as well as detailed Duty Sheets to be studied by anyone with sufficient self-confidence to volunteer for a Staff Training Course:

> Bell codes should be given slowly and regularly. It is confusing – and not smart – to send codes too quickly. Signalmen should memorize all of these Bell Codes and be thoroughly conversant with their meanings
> ONLY THE YARDMASTER MAY FIT AND REMOVE PINS FROM VEHICLES.

Still, as the Foreword to the book says, 'These Rules and Regulations and other items . . . have been designed so that members will be able to run the M.M.R. with a maximum of enjoyment and as much akin to the prototype as possible.'

And, there are other consolations. Those tough enough to complete the Staff Training Course satisfactorily, the Rule Book says, 'will be promoted to Train Controller and issued with a suitable certificate.' To earn one of those, at Melbourne, is a real accolade.

51 The Macclesfield Model Railway Group have re-built part of their 3 mm. scale layout. The original plan is shown on 154. The Banktop signal cabin and environs are illustrated here.

11 Track

When the Romans occupied north-western Europe and Britain nearly two thousand years ago, the roads they made were paved with flat stones, leaving, to accommodate their carriage wheels, ruts that were just four feet eight inches apart. When tracks were first laid for the early, primitive colliery railways, the distance between the inner edges of the lines was approximately four feet eight inches. It is probable, then, that the Roman road-makers were indirectly responsible for the gauge – 4 feet $8\frac{1}{2}$ inches – that has since been used for railway lines in so many parts of the world.

In 1776, a wagon-way that was to play an important part in railway history was built in the north of England. It was intended to carry coal from the Duke of Norfolk's mine to Sheffield, the nearest town. The men who had been making a living, up to that time, by carting the coal were unwilling to lose their jobs. So they tore up the wooden rails and made bonfires with them.

The Duke's colliery manager, John Curr, was a resourceful man. He had the track re-laid, using, to discourage further sabotage, iron rails spiked down to heavy stone cross-track supports – the kind that would be known as ties or sleepers. More, he had trucks made with unflanged wheels that could, if necessary, be drawn by horses along the ordinary highways. To keep these trucks on the rails for which they were primarily intended, Curr had flanges added to the sides of the rails. Track of this kind became known as plate way. Trevithick used plate rails when he ran his historic tram engine in 1804 .

Rails of a more sophisticated kind – those held in the special fittings known as chairs, which, in their turn, were fastened to cross-track ties or sleepers – were first used in a wagon-way built by Thomas Barnes in 1797. This, too, was a notable occasion in railway history, for rails of this sort were in general use in most parts of the world for the next hundred and fifty years (and, in some places, can still be found, giving excellent service).

When the first railways intended for the transport of passengers were being constructed, the track was laid by contracting companies. Often, the contractors would collect and store the necessary materials at their own depôts, which might be some distance from

e Gauge N track made by
nold is shown in this commercial
out. It is typical of the realistic
del track manufactured today.

the nearest point of the new line. To get these materials from the depôt to the site, the contractor would usually lay a temporary service track. .To avoid confusion with this soon-to-be-removed line, the railway under construction would be referred to as the permanent way. The term is used in many parts of the world to this day.

In any model railway layout, the track or permanent way is of prime importance. The requirements it has to fulfil fall neatly into two categories – it must not spoil, by its own appearance, the appearance of the models that run on it, and it has to allow the best performance that can possibly be achieved with them.

It will be most convenient, perhaps, to deal first with the track's appearance. This is one of the most discussed topics in the whole of railway modelling, since getting track to look unobtrusively right is one of the hardest tasks that faces any layout-maker.

And that brings up at once the question of scale. If track is not made exactly to scale, no model that runs on it can ever look entirely convincing. Most commercially produced track has to be strong if it is to survive even a little rough handling. In giving their track sufficient strength, many manufacturers are tempted to ignore the original fine proportions of the prototype, making the rails over-size, coarsening the attachments, and filling up, for purposes of support, any under-rail gaps with thin but visible membranes that give the finished product at once an air of artificiality.

In striving for absolute truth, the perfectionist is more likely to want to build his own track than to use any that he can buy ready-made. Hand-building will take him a lot longer, but he will be able to work to the closest possible limits, and will be able to match his wheel and track standards exactly, as well. Modellers who habitually use commercially produced track (and they are the vast majority) will normally be content to find and use some universal track system that will accept as many different wheel contours as possible. This may be convenient, as it allows a layout-owner to run models made by a number of manufacturers on a common set of lines. It cannot, in the nature of things, produce an absolutely truthful representation of one particular line, which, as has been pointed out, is the normal aim of the perfectionist.

The first commercially produced track that looked anything like the real thing came (as so much else in railway modelling) as a result of the ceaseless striving for truth of Wenman Bassett-Lowke. Soon after he started to market his momentous true-to-prototype locomotives at the beginnning of this century, he saw the need for track that was sufficiently realistic for them to run on. So, he came up with his Lowko track, in which hollow rails were held in slide-on chairs that were spiked to wooden sleepers. More, for those modellers who were intent on reproducing every detail found in the full-size railways of the period he brought out an excellent track that he called, quite straightforwardly, Scale Model Permanent Way. This had solid rails resting in cast chairs. The rails were held tightly in place in the chairs (as in real life) by hardwood keys.

Today, the railway modeller is offered a bewildering variety of commercially produced tracks, manufacturers in at least five countries making and exporting enough to satisfy all usual demands. The beginner has to decide whether to use rigid, sectional track – the kind usually supplied with model train sets – or one of the modern flexible track systems, such as the excellent Peco Streamline, made by the Pritchard Patent Product Company, of Seaton, Devon, England. The latter are rapidly increasing in popularity.

The sectional tracks sold nowadays are, in the main, less visually disturbing than the old tinplate track they have largely replaced. Tinplate track normally bore little resemblance to any real-life prototype – for one thing, the only function of the metal sleepers was to keep the rails the right distance apart, and they were spaced out, for reasons of economy in manufacture, at the widest practicable intervals. While few modern sectional tracks look more than partly convincing, most do have at least a reasonable number of sleepers, and the rails in some are not too wildly out of scale.

The flexible tracks on the market today are mostly provided with nickel-silver rails. (Perfectionists paint or spray the metal a dingy, rusty brown, polishing the colour off the upper surfaces afterwards, so that only those parts that are to come into contact with the train wheels will be bright, as in prototype rails.) The sleepers, chairs and spacing bars are usually made of plastic, coloured to resemble the prototype, more or less. A few manufacturers, such as Messrs Wrenn, use fibre sleepers, which are especially easy to glue or pin to a baseboard.

Laying flexible track is a comparatively easy job. The best results are obtained when the track is not laid directly on to a baseboard, but on to some kind of underlay such as a thin foam-rubber sheeting, or cork, which will provide a certain amount of resilience as well as helping to absorb any disproportionate and unrealistic noise. The track is easy to cut and trim exactly to size, and it can be bent to suit any reasonable track plan without difficulty. It can be fixed in position with glue or with small track pins or brads. In layouts that are to be portable, this has to be done so thoroughly that the track is practically immovable, but in all layouts that are to be relatively static the track may be secured sufficiently with a very few pins.

Railway track consists normally of at least four features. Besides the rails, chairs, and sleepers already mentioned, there is also the

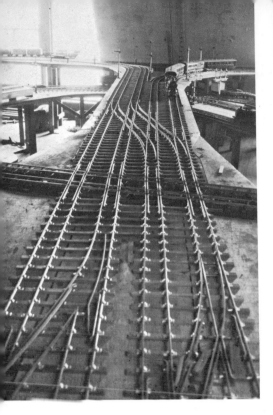

156 *Left – Gauge O track laid
by Bassett-Lowke for the British
Empire Exhibition, Glasgow in
1938*

157 *Right – A model engine yard,
showing the realism that can be
obtained with the correct use of
track ballast.*

ballast, which is some hard granular material that helps to grip
and hold the sleepers in position. It is carefully chosen to allow
moisture to drain away from the track. Of these four ingredients,
the two last are of particular concern to modellers who want their
work to be realistic.

Prototype sleepers are usually made from wood (almost always
so, in the older railways) or from concrete. Wooden sleepers are
normally treated with creosote or some other proved preservative
which gives them their unmistakable colour and texture. This
special quality of surface is hard to reproduce in miniature sleepers
made of card, fibre or plastic. Some manufacturers have worked
hard to achieve realism in these substitute materials, but wood, in
spite of all their efforts, has been found by many of the most
successful modellers in the world to be the ideal material for
representing wood!

Ballast, too, tends to have textures – if not colours – that are
difficult to reproduce in miniature. Most of the substitute materials
sold by the trade have grains that are too large or too small for the
track with which they are to be associated, or particles – such as
those produced by maw seed or crumbled cork – that are, even at
a quick glance, the wrong shape. Mixed with adhesive, and slapped
on a baseboard, many of these makeshifts tend to resemble cold
porridge. Some patient and punctilious modellers have found no
better way of representing ballast than by surrounding their tracks
with the real stuff – granite chippings or local gravel crushed until

the bits can be passed through a sieve with a mesh of a suitable size.

A horse can turn left or right at any stage of a forward movement, as its rider wishes. So can an automobile, at the whim of its driver. A train is less easily manoeuvred. It must run resolutely along its pre-ordained tracks until it comes to the ingeniously contrived junctions that allow it to change its direction of travel. At each of these junctions, there will normally be found one of those perennially interesting items of equipment known in different parts of the world as switches or points.

The standard form of prototype switch is made up principally of two movable pointed rails that are set between the running rails. In some switches, these movable rails are fastened together by means of bars of metal known as stretcher bars. These bars ensure that both the rails to which they are attached will move, when they are required to, the same distance and at exactly the same time. In other switches, the pointed rails are arranged to move independently. (This may be used as a precautionary measure, where a siding joins a main line, to ensure that any train that attempts to move on to the main line when the switches and

signals are not correctly set will be de-railed.) The most compli-cated prototype switches involve the use of a number of pointed rails, each of which may have to be moved independently.

The majority of commercially made model switches are, basically, combinations of straight running rails and curved turn-out rails of even radius. In this respect they will be found to have been simplified slightly from the true prototype form for ease of manufacture, for if full-size track is examined closely, the curve of a diverging rail will be seen to change to straight before it crosses the straight running rail, and it will continue to be straight for a short distance after the crossing before it becomes curved again. This effect is striven for by the perfectionist, who usually decides to hand-build his switches for the sake of exactness.

An important element in a switch – the angle made by the two rails at the point of crossing – is known as a frog. Model switches are usually made and sold to conform to some particular frog number, which indicates the angle of separation to be seen between the diverging rail and the straight rail immediately after the frog. Thus, a Number 10 set of points will have a very gradual diver-gence, and will be used for high speed working, while a Number 4

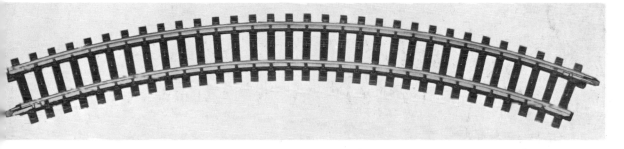

58 Four examples of track sections a Gauge HO commercially manu-actured to exacting standards. above, left, a straight rail ; right, a urved rail. Left, a point (or turn-ut) ; right, a double point (or ouble slip switch). The latter two re remote controlled.

set of points will show a greater angle, and will be used only for diverting slower trains into sidings. An express train, travelling fast, is liable to be de-railed by too sudden a change of direction. (Speed restriction posts, placed at the approaches of junctions, are familiar features of the railway landscape in both prototype and model forms.) Some manufacturers of railway models now offer switches with built-in devices that will throw the points automatically if an approaching train has the switch set against it.

The performance of any model train depends on certain qualities in the track laid down for it to run on, just as the reliability of the prototype depends on the excellence (or otherwise) of the permanent way. One of the biggest items of expenditure to be met by any railway company is that incurred in the maintenance of its lines. The railway modeller has to be just as vigilant, even if his financial outlay is (fortunately for him) reduced proportionately.

First, he must see that his track is of exactly the right gauge, and that it remains that way, without getting wider or narrower throughout its whole length. Templates can be bought (or easily made) that will control the track width with no possibility of error.

Then, he must see that there is no cross-wind in his track – this may sound technical, but it only means that both rails must be at exactly the same level, in relation to each other, throughout the length of the track. If the baseboard is as level and as rigid as it should be, this should happen automatically. If the baseboard has warped badly, it should, where possible, be scrapped, for no truly level track can be laid on it without a seemingly endless amount of adjustment and packing. Less serious deficiencies are usually palliated by the compensating axles found on most contemporary rolling stock.

Next, the modeller has to make sure that there are no sudden angles or changes of direction in the track. If these 'dog-legs' are allowed to remain, they will inevitably produce erratic running and, probably, a high accident rate.

This is the factor, more than any other, that is liable to affect adversely the appearance of a miniature layout as well as the performance of the models that are worked on it. Few, if any, real railways are compounded of straight lines and sharp curves. Long flowing curves and relatively short straight stretches are much more typical. Modellers who aim at realism try to incorporate these in their layouts. If such modellers are forced, by the restricted area in which they have to work, to fix their track in curves of unnaturally severe radii, they usually manage to keep such curves out of sight in tunnels or behind some specially contrived natural feature. What the eye does not see, runs an old proverb, the heart does not grieve over!

9 Superior model track for a ndon North Eastern layout with alistic sleepers. Commercial track n often be adapted to make it more ue-to-life.

12 Stations and Other Buildings

The earliest railways, used only for carrying coal, ore, stone, and other heavy commodities, needed no special buildings.

When passengers were first carried, no additional arrangements were made for their comfort. They were expected to wait, to buy food, and drink, and to use the toilet facilities, when these were necessary, at the hotels and inns nearest to the line.

Later, when passenger traffic increased, the public hostelries were no longer able to cope with the growing demands made on their services. The railway companies, compelled by competition to study the needs of their customers, were forced to provide buildings of their own to accommodate them. A few of these early station buildings – at Liverpool Road, Manchester, England, and at Mount Clare, Baltimore, Maryland, in the United States, for example – are still in existence.

The very first specially built railway stations were little more than crude wooden shelters – they could have been mistaken quite easily for rough farm sheds or the primitive cabins that were being hastily erected in newly explored territories in so many parts of the world.

Then, the railway engineers woke up to the fact that their stations could be more useful than this, and they called in architects to plan buildings in which tickets could be sold, luggage handled, and all the short-term needs of the passengers satisfied. Wherever possible, the railway staff too were to be accommodated in the new, and grander, stations.

When a station was to serve a thickly populated area, it would often be provided with a large airy extension, or canopy, that would shelter the tracks and the ground to each side of them. These extensions, which were usually called sheds, would normally consist largely of glass, so that the areas where the passengers waited for, and alighted from, trains would be as fully lighted as possible.

Where trains were not expected to serve so many people, the canopies just described would have been an unnecessary expense. So, smaller canopies or verandahs were added instead to the station buildings to give some shelter to the people waiting for trains,

A view of Kirtley station in Midland Railway Exhibit in Derby Municipal Museum.

161 Left – An exceptionally realist American *lighted freight station from Tyco.*

162 Below – A model of the engine shed of the 1874 Pipitea station, New Zealand, made by Frank Roberts.

163 Right – Weathering has given the lime loading hoppers on David Jenkinson's 4 mm. scale layout a look of complete realism.

164 Below, right – Whitney K. Towers has modelled some superb buildings for his Alturas and Lone Pine layout. The Bulline Packers' shed and live-stock pens are shown.

and to the station staff. Usually, these verandahs would need some kind of support, but the most obvious method of providing this – with upright pillars – was rarely satisfactory, since pillars tend to cause obstruction in crowded places, and, in any case, no upright support could be placed near the track or it would be liable to be struck by the carriage doors. So, the men who made the early stations were forced to experiment, and the ingenuity, charm and occasional eccentricity of their various designs make these buildings endlessly fascinating to railway modellers who want their layouts to have a pronounced individuality.

The early stations did not have platforms at all, only the largest having special 'parades' constructed that would save the passengers from lengthy waits on damp ground. The advantages of raising

165 Above – The Rico station for a Gauge O layout, manufactured by Pola.

166 Below – The station facade in the Derby Municipal Museum Midland Railway layout (see also p. 186). All the model buildings in this layout are copies of existing buildings or were made from the plans of demolished buildings.

67 *A more modern set of buildings shown in this model of the Sheffield Midland station made by the Sheffield Model Railway enthusiasts for their Gauge OO layout.*

these parades so that the passengers could enter and leave the carriages without having to climb up and down steep ladderways soon became obvious to the railway architects of many countries. In some countries – France and the United States are examples – stations without elevated platforms are by no means rare.

Only an exceptional modeller will set himself the task of reproducing in miniature one of the larger railway stations built during the nineteenth century. (The sort of person who does may well be a man who has missed his vocation as an architect, and who satisfies, by his hobby, the frustrations he hardly even recognizes.) Many of these stations are as pretentious and imposing as any public building put up to emphasize municipal grandeur. They were the by-products of the financing company's desire to impress.

They were put up partly as demonstrations of pride – for the construction of an important new line was a memorable achievement – and partly for commercial reasons. A spanking new station was a most valuable advertisement!

The railway modeller who wishes to own a comparatively small station that will serve satisfactorily as a single component of his model railway layout has four alternatives from which to choose – he can buy a ready-to-assemble kit; he can make a station that reproduces an existing or historic prototype; he can make one to his own, free-lance, design; or he can buy one ready-made.

Many commercially produced kits offer a number of components printed on card. The buildings that can be made from these kits are usually adequate, but they tend, understandably, to look a little stereotyped. They often appear, too, to have been planned on an unrealistically economical basis. One set of kits now selling by the thousand produces track-side churches that would not be large enough, if they were actually built full-size, to hold more than two dozen people.

The railway modeller who decides to make his own models of stations and other buildings, basing them on existing or historic prototypes, has first to do a certain amount of research, so that his replicas will have the same authentic quality as the locomotives and rolling stock with which they are to be combined. Many modellers get a great amount of pleasure from visiting the buildings they intend to reproduce – photographing, sketching, and taking exact measurements. One particularly meticulous model-maker reckons that he may need to take as many as two hundred and fifty photographs of even a small group of buildings before he can be sure that he has enough information to be able to work confidently at home from his dimensioned sketches.

Unless he has had considerable experience of woodwork or metalwork, the modeller setting out to make buildings is generally recommended to choose cardboard as his basic material. Almost any card can be used, as long as it can be cut cleanly with a sharp craft knife, and as long as it will be reasonably rigid when it has been made to the required size. Walls cut from card look best if they are made up from two identical pieces, having, between them, a gap into which can be fitted bits of glass or transparent plastic to represent glazing for windows and other sources of light. Cornices, mouldings, buttresses, and other features that may be difficult to reproduce with card may be cut from strips of balsa wood, spruce, or one of the other easily trimmed materials favoured by model-makers. The comparatively cheap material known as styrene sheet is proving invaluable for window frames, doors, and other details that need to be carefully shaped.

The model-maker who wants to make reproductions of stations

The coaling station at Alturas is one of the many fine buildings modelled by Whitney K. Towers for his Gauge HO Alturas and Lone Pine Railroad.

Overleaf, several firms manufacture buildings for use with various standard gauges. Here is a selection for use on a European layout.

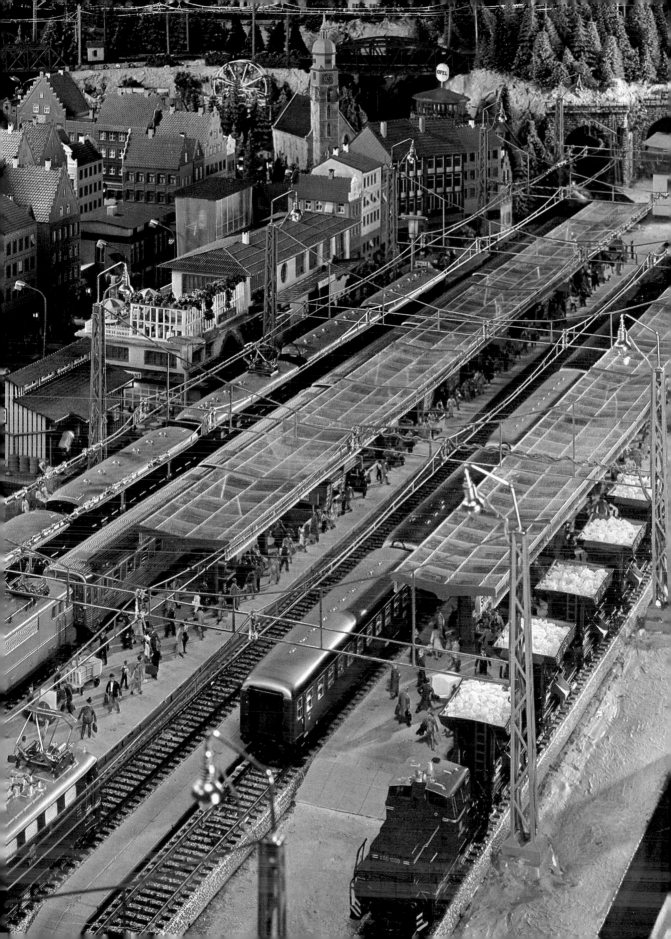

and other buildings (or buildings to his own, free-lance designs) from a more permanent material than card will turn, usually, to wood. Thin, resin-bonded plywood sheeting is often chosen, and so are spruce, some tropical and other easily worked woods. The softer grades of balsa wood can be cut to shape almost as easily as cheese, but many model-makers consider that these lack the necessary strength. The tools needed for making miniature buildings from wood are few – a metal straight-edge and a metal square are useful for drawing out the parts; a small veneer saw is ideal for working from thin sheets and for cutting larger pieces to size; a sharp knife is essential; small needle files and glasspaper are needed for the finishing touches. Parts may be assembled with any suitable adhesive – the impact glues sold today for household woodwork purposes will make satisfactory joints without any of the long setting periods that can hold up work with infuriating delays.

A large number of railway buildings in many different parts of the world are made with bricks, and others are made from stone. Both these can be imitated quite easily in a model made from card or wood if the exposed wall surfaces are covered with one of the lining papers specially printed for the purpose. The most important point to watch, once again, is that of scale – if the bricks or stones shown in a printed paper are larger or smaller than real bricks or stones, reduced proportionately, could possibly be, the whole building will look wrong, however carefully it may have been modelled in other respects.

Each of the aspects of railway modelling in this book will attract some enthusiasts, and fail to interest others. In each activity, there will be special opportunities for some particularly talented modellers to exercise their skills. No branch of railway modelling offers greater scope to the virtuoso with an eye for almost microscopic detail than the construction of miniature buildings.

One of the most painstaking craftsmen in the world is Australian-born Roye England, who is the quiet but purposeful founder of the Pendon Museum Trust team. Under his leadership some extraordinary miniature landscapes are being created, with the appropriate buildings. These landscapes are intended to preserve into the foreseeable future the memory of some particularly beautiful rural districts of England, with their railways, which are being altered out of all recognition even as the Pendon models are being made.

Roye England and his helpers are working to a scale of 4 millimetres (0.16 inch) to 1 foot – that is, a scale ratio of 1 :76. Building a miniature replica of a small group of cottages may take a member of the happy team as much as seven thousand hours. As each earns a living, during normal working hours, at some other job, this

Above, a commercial girder bridge compared with, below, an old stone bridge modelled by David Jenkinson

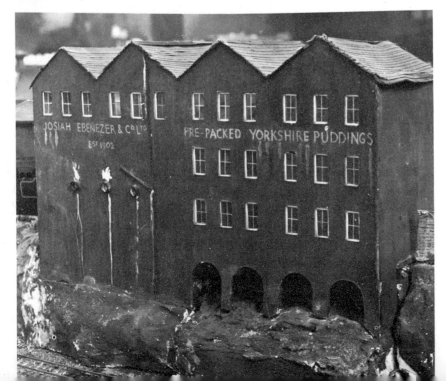

part of the great undertaking alone will take them an incalculable
number of years.

The lengths to which devoted craftsmen of this kind will go
can be profitably studied at Pendon. There, the tiny and quite
perfect buildings are made of fine quality white card. This must
not be too hard in its surface, nor inclined to split. The textures of
the walls are reproduced by careful scoring, the outlines of each
tiny brick or stone being pressed into the card with a special
scriber. Seven thousand bricks have been delineated in this way,
Roye England has calculated, in the walls of a single small chapel.
Coloured with artists' water colours, often using several coats, the
scored card is made to look like weathered brick, stone, cement or
wood so exactly that it could be easily mistaken for the prototype
material. Each slate or tile is cut from paper or very thin card, and
these, before being laid, are coloured individually to match those
on the original roof – there are 4,375 of them in the roof of a single

farmhouse. Any slate or tile that has been displaced in a prototype roof will be reproduced with loving care in its new, fortuitous position by the Pendon enthusiasts.

When the walls of the Pendon buildings are near completion, the tiny windows are fitted into place. Either mica or real glass may be used for these, as they have (like everything else at Pendon) to be a perfect reproduction, in miniature, of the original, even their thickness must be exactly right and to scale. So, microscope slide covers – about $\frac{1}{100}$ inch thick, or thin – are used. In cottage windows the glazing bars are made from housewives' sewing cotton. Many of the cottages are thatched with human hair, which can be made to look convincingly like straw. Chinese hair is used, since this happens to be conveniently straight. The hair, which is black before it arrives at Pendon, is first bleached and then dyed to the correct colour, after which it is sent to the University at Leeds to be mothproofed. Thatching is done in much the same way as in the original, packing small bundles closely up the roof, trimming, and pegging on the runners – using entomological pins for the pegs.

For every modeller who is prepared to go to the same trouble as the dedicated men at Pendon, there must be many thousands who will be more than satisfied with the excellent stations, freight depôts, engine sheds, signal cabins, water towers and other buildings

172 Tyco have produced this Gauge HO railroad crossing and shanty. It is automatic in the sense that when the locomotive reaches the track section, the door opens and the signalman emerges and remains in position until the whole train has cleared the crossing.

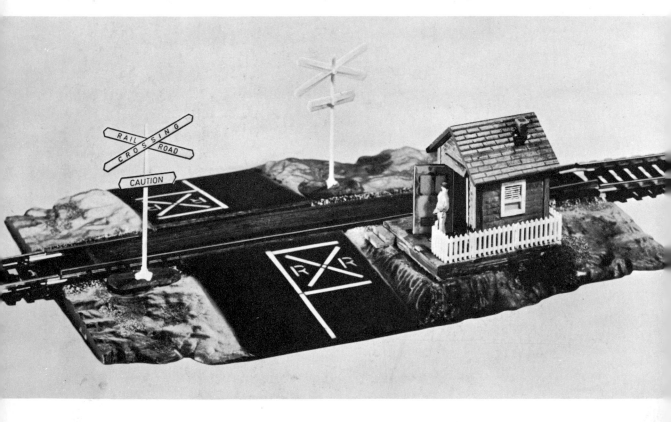

marketed now by Märklin, Rivarossi, Rovex, and several other firms of comparable standing. Märklin (to take one example only) offers a splendid all-automatic level crossing unit. This incorporates a crossing-keeper's hut, equipped so that interior lighting can be easily fitted, warning cross signs, and two barriers that are operated electro-magnetically. The barriers close as soon as a train runs on to the track contact section in front of the crossing, and open again automatically when the train leaves the last track contact section after the crossing.

Reasonably faithful reproductions of existing structures as these commercial models usually are, they are unlikely in one respect to look exactly like the prototypes on which they were based – almost certainly they will appear, when they are purchased, temptingly clean and tidy. Most real-life railway buildings get a weathered look very shortly after they are brought into service – paint becomes slightly yellow with age, a film of dust soon starts to settle in all but a few abnormally clean places, and tyre marks appear on roads. The immediate surroundings of buildings on the railways, too, are rarely neat and entirely free from rubbish. Fortunately, these slight deviations from a natural appearance can soon be remedied by an enterprising modeller who has a set of water colours or poster paints and a fine brush. It is much easier to make a model look realistically soiled than it is to clean one up!

173 This model crossing has two barriers and a guard's shed, designed to accept interior lighting. The barriers close automatically as soon as a train runs on to the track control section in front of the barriers, and open again when the train has left the last section of control track after the crossing.

13 Signals

In most spheres of human activity, there are some processes that are put into operation because they are needed, or so that a closely integrated series of operations may run more smoothly, and there are some that are initiated and carried out purely for effect. In the railway modelling world the most unnecessary aspect is surely that of signalling. Real-life train drivers depend on signals to tell them whether they can advance safely, or alternatively, should remain at rest and await further instruction. But there are no fingernail-size drivers watching for signals in the miniature trains that rush in complete safety round the best regulated miniature tracks. The tiny signals that move, or light up, and appear to control these trains are quite superfluous, and are installed only to make the model conform more exactly to the prototype. In spite of their uselessness, though, model railway signals can provide the man who operates them with an extraordinary amount of excitement and pleasure. And is not that typical of so many of life's most splendid delights?

The earliest trains, drawn by locomotives driven by steam power, were generally regarded as dangerous monsters. Propelling themselves along recently laid tracks at speeds that were more than twice as fast as a man could run, their astonishing momentum could carry them into incalculable disaster if some behind-the-times obstacle such as a horse or a cow had settled down for a quiet sleep on the line. So, every surveyable stretch had to be guarded by a policeman, armed with one of the most compulsive – at that time – of all alarm signals: a flag.

The first fixed railway signals were erected, as far as we know, in 1834 on the Liverpool and Manchester line. Each consisted of an upright post to which was attached, on pivots, a board that was exactly the shape of a railway policeman's flag. When the way ahead was blocked, the boards would be turned outwards, at right angles to the track, so that they resembled the raised flags they had been designed to replace. When the way ahead was clear, the boards would be pushed round so that they were parallel to the track, and therefore hardly visible. Each signal needed a man to operate it, so the new system brought no saving of manpower.

4 A very fine model set of English semaphore signals made Bassett-Lowke.

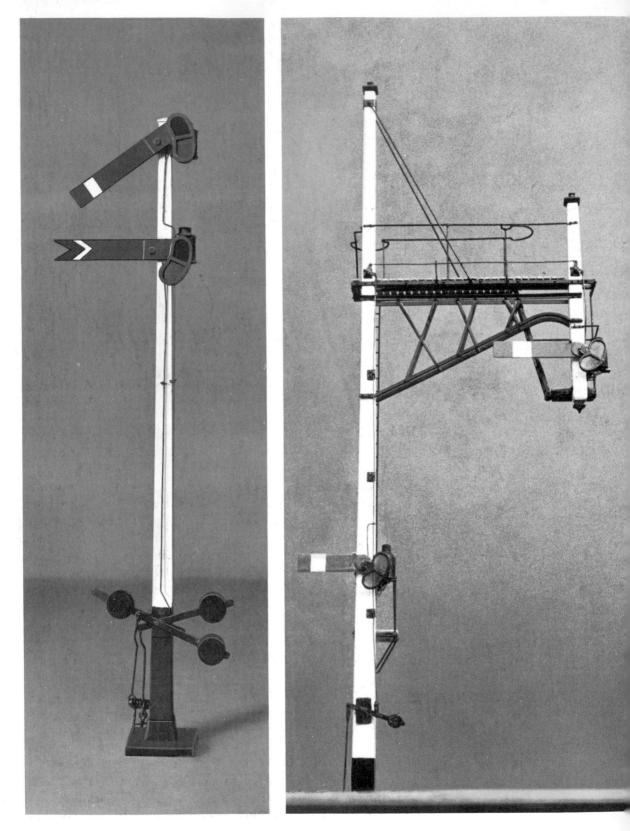

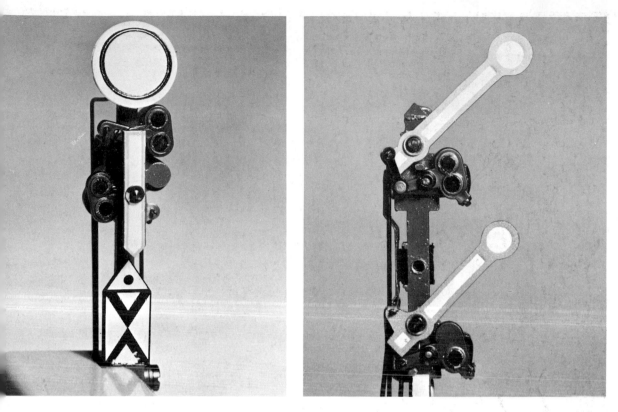

75 Far left – Another semaphore signal manufactured by Bassett-Lowke.

76 Left – G. Pember modelled his up home signal in 7 mm scale; also shows a platform starter.

77 Above – A Märklin distant signal (this is placed 1,000 metres ahead of the home signal); it has fixed disc and movable arm as well as lights.

78 Above, right – a home signal in the 'proceed slowly' position. The lights are green over amber, and like the whole Märklin model signal range this is fully illuminated.

The London and Croydon Railway, which was opened in 1839, was the first to use disc signals. In the London and Croydon's version, red discs that signified STOP could be turned on pivots so that they were at right angles to the track, and therefore would be easily seen by the drivers of approaching trains. Two years later, the Great Western Railway Company borrowed the London and Croydon Company's idea, and improved on it. The warning discs were placed on high posts, so that they could be seen from a considerable distance. More, a flag-like crossbar was added to each disc, and at right angles to it. In their system, a disc turned into full view gave the message GO, the crossbar being used to order STOP. The new method found immediate favour and was widely copied in France and other European countries.

The chief weakness of the early systems of signalling lay in the crudity of the methods by which the movement of trains was controlled, each policeman being instructed to enforce a stated time interval after the passage of one train before he allowed through the next. Having no communication with the next policeman along the line, he usually had no way of knowing whether or not the last train to pass had broken down in the section immediately ahead – he just had to keep one eye on his clock and hope for the best. Even when the electric telegraph was introduced, it was only to connect the more important main line stations. The

haphazard methods of early railway operation may be nicely judged from this extract from Daniel Gooch's 'Regulations' for March 1840. The order concerns the sign to be hoisted by rope and pulley outside Reading Station: 'A Signal Ball will be seen at the entrance to Reading Station when the Line is right for the Train to go in. If the Ball is not visible, the Train must not pass it.'

The introduction of semaphore signals in 1841 – again, on the the London and Croydon Railway – was a highly significant event for all modellers interested in the history of railways, since signals of this type, based on contemporary naval practice, were to play for many years a vital part in the railway scene.

At first, the signals applying to two or more parallel tracks would be mounted one above the other, on the same post. At junctions, and in places where there were a large number of tracks, this could be confusing and dangerous. The semaphores were arranged on the principle 'Left hand track at the top of the post, right hand track at the bottom.' An engine driver approaching one of these multiple signals would have to read down the semaphores until he came to one that applied to his train, or until he thought he had. Eventually, the railway companies were persuaded to arrange their signals in a more sensible manner on horizontal brackets or gantries. Many of these were very large and impressive structures, but they present a considerable challenge to the railway modeller

179 Kirtley signal box in the Midland Railway layout in the Derby Municipal Museum.

who wishes to reproduce them, since they were constructed mainly from many small and comparatively slender components.

Two years after the first semaphore signals were introduced, the man who had been primarily responsible for them – Charles Hutton Gregory – constructed a central lever frame for switches and signals that incorporated a rudimentary safety device. In 1856, a Mr J. Saxby concentrated a number of switch and signal levers in one cabin, and interlocked them there, showing that all the switches and signals of a junction or station could be worked in harmony, and without danger. Many arrangements were invented to fulfil this purpose, but in 1870 Messrs J. J., J. J. F. and W. J. Stevens patented a tappet interlocking mechanism which practically superseded all others and became the basis for approved signalling systems in most parts of the world.

All measures taken to ensure safe running on the railways since the middle of the nineteenth century depend, to some extent, on the block section system. In organizing this, every stretch of line is divided into a number of block sections. Each section is under the control of a signalman whose duty it is to see that no more than one train is on his section of the main line at any one time. The system is still operated, the principle remaining valid even where the old semaphores have been replaced by more modern devices.

For some years after the start of the general move towards greater realism in railway modelling at the beginning of this century, model signals and signalling remained in a relatively neglected state. There were a few beautifully made model semaphores on the market – Märklin was particularly proud of its signals in which dummy lanterns could be raised or lowered by means of chain and crank mechanisms, and there were others that had working miniature oil lanterns. All these were sadly out of scale, however, and looked ridiculous when seen near one of the new, true-to-prototype model trains.

Then, in 1910, true-to-scale model signals were produced and marketed by Wenman Bassett-Lowke. The quality of these models was immediately recognized, and not only in the miniature field, for the directors of the London and North Western Railway Company soon invited Bassett-Lowke to make for them a model signalling instruction table. This was to show a block section of track, and was to include a junction and sidings. The whole was to be controlled, as a similar, full-size section of track would have been, by fully interlocked signals and switches, with working block telegraphs in miniature. The Railway Company's commission was to have far-reaching effects. By their action they had demonstrated publicly that a model has not only a hobby value but that it may have an important instructional purpose. No amount of reading matter or of explanatory talking can have the clarity or impres-

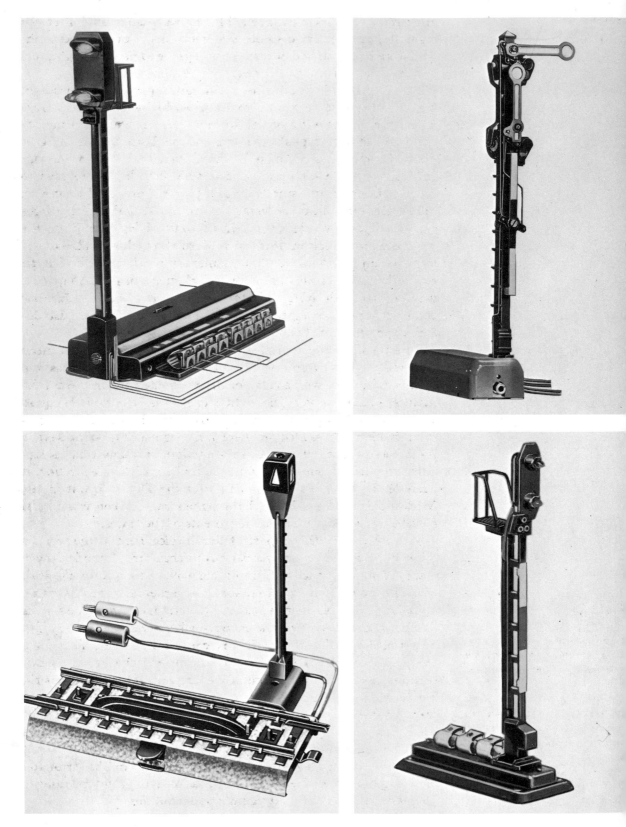

siveness of a working model. The railwayman studying at the signalling table learned to observe every detail of the operations that were being carried out before his eyes, and he was taught, too, how to react quickly and correctly to his observations.

Modern signalling systems are usually operated by means of bright lights – some signals that are worked automatically from a distance can, in addition, make trains stop or start according to the light shown. Signals that depend on light can be roughly divided into a number of different categories. There are colour light signals, in which red, green and yellow lights are used to convey the messages stop, proceed, proceed prepared to stop at next signal and other necessary instructions, and position light signals. There are signals in which rows of lights indicate the route is clear; signals in which rows of white or yellow bulbs convey information in upper quadrant semaphore fashion (a horizontal row of lights ordering stop, a row at 45° suggesting caution, and a vertical row indicating safe to proceed); and signals that use coloured lights, arranged in positions similar to those just described, adding, in this way, an extra margin of safety.

The gradual disappearance of the semaphore signal and other obsolete devices from the real railways of the world has not pleased modellers with a taste for the antiquated and an eye for the picturesque. However, the light signals that are now being so widely installed in prototype systems allow the modeller who is even moderately skilled at electrical engineering to achieve a remarkable degree of realism in operation. In many famous layouts, such as the outdoor one in the Swissminiatur Exhibition at Meilide, by the Lake of Lugano, and the Dutch layout in the Madurodam at The Hague, light signals can be seen working in perfect conformity with the movements of the trains.

As with every other aspect of the development of the world's railways, the great commercial manufacturers of models have managed to keep pace with rapid changes in the prototype field. Märklin – to name only one company – markets a range of exciting model signals that are linked exactly with train control. The signals can be placed anywhere the layout-maker wishes – to the right or left of the track, on straight stretches or on curves. They have baseplates that enable them to be firmly attached to the track sections, and they are operated by electro-magnetic mechanisms. These devices make it possible for the indications of all signals as well as the setting of all switches, or points, to be shown on distant control panels. Anyone who has the chance to direct, from a single remote vantage point, the running of model trains on a layout that has been fully equipped with signals of this kind is fortunate. He will get many of the pleasures of up-to-date prototype railway operation without the contingent responsibilities.

80 Above, left – A model light home signal.

81 Above, right – A model home signal with two coupled semaphore arms and signal lights.

82 Below, left – An uncoupler light standard. The light in this remote control fitting is illuminated when the uncoupler track is energized.

83 Below, right – A model by Fleischmann of a light signal.

14 Landscape

To many railway modellers, a layout consisting of track, buildings and rolling stock is of little interest unless some thought has been given to the landscape through which the railway runs. The only layouts that are really satisfactory to modellers who think this way are those in which there is a pleasing balance between the carefully regulated workings of a man-made transport system and the naturally formed land by which it is surrounded.

It is easy to understand this attitude. Every railway, in real life, has a geographical setting with a character of its own. We remember our railway journeys – if we are not too obsessed by the machines that are carrying us to notice – by the fields, plains, rivers, lakes, valleys and mountains that we have passed, or that have appeared to pass us, on the way.

The relationship between a railway track and the landscape through which it passes is never accidental. The surface of the ground will almost certainly have been changed considerably with the coming of the railway engineers: embankments will have been raised and cuttings will have been excavated to carry the track with as few marked changes of level as possible over un-dulating country; hills and mountains may have to be pierced with tunnels; viaducts may have had to be built to carry the track over deep valleys, and bridges to carry it across rivers. Every mile will tell some interesting story of a surveyor's or constructor's skill, of the power that men have to control their environment and turn it to their own uses.

So, the modeller who wishes to show a railway, or part of one, in its landscape setting has first to do a certain amount of research. He will study the structure of the ground, carefully observing the rock formations, the level alluvial surfaces and other characteristic features. He will note the principles that may have influenced the railway engineers when they were faced with the problem of deciding between alternative methods of circumventing obstacles. One of these determining factors may be the purpose of the line. All other things being equal, a main line, having to take faster traffic, will be made up of easier curves and gradients than a secondary or branch line. In all probability, these basic differences

84 John Allen's landscape in his Gorre and Daphetid layout is remarkably realistic. The water is plastic, cast in place.

will in turn affect the nature of the engineering works. A trunk route may well need much more substantial earth movement if it is to be given a fast alignment. These, and similar factors, have to be borne constantly in mind by the modeller who wishes his work to be completely convincing.

Next, the modeller setting out to realise a railway in its natural surroundings will have to define its boundaries – a miniature landscape must necessarily have a beginning, some side extremities and an end, it cannot go on indefinitely into the distance as a real landscape can. Some modellers are quite content if their layouts finish suddenly, at the baseboard edges. Others are extremely skilful at devising backgrounds – either painted back-cloths, or photographs enlarged until they are big enough to cover walls – into which the adjoining land forms can be fused so deceptively that only the keenest-eyed observers can pick out the joins. When looking at a layout that has been presented as artistically as this, the spectator may be quite unconscious that he is not, in fact, looking at a limitless expanse of country. Crudely painted white clouds on a harsh blue sky backcloth, on the other hand, can immediately destroy all sense of illusion.

Inside the boundaries, the landscape modeller has next to find the most suitable positions for his principal land forms. The shape and size of his mountains, hills and plateaux may have been pre-determined, or virtually so, by the dimensions and outlines of his supporting surfaces. Usually it is most satisfactory if the baseboard plan, the geographical scheme and the track layout are arrived at at one and the same time.

Next, the high ground has to be built up on the baseboard. Where the track is to be and where buildings are to stand must be firm and level. Everywhere else can be rough, or jagged, or gently curved, exactly as the surfaces of the prototype landscape would be.

There are several quick ways of building up high ground. Some model-makers cut pieces of plywood or hardboard to the required profiles, afterwards fixing them together with glues or screws so that they will stand firmly on the baseboard. Other modellers build up their land forms to the nearest approximate levels with cardboard boxes or cartons. Others again, mindful of the fact that all supports will be hidden, are content to use balls of crumpled newspaper.

Modellers who try to build up solid land forms with mixtures of plaster and sawdust, home-made pulp, or any other enthusiastic-ally contrived modelling compound often find that they have on their baseboards masses of soggy, porridge-like material that they have thoroughly enjoyed playing with, but which will not dry out for weeks.

Above, European mountain scenery is shown on the model layout of the St. Gotthard Railway.

Below, part of Giant Canyon in John Allen's Gauge HO layout of 'The Gorre and Daphetid Railroad' At this point his scenery goes down to floor level.

Overleaf, the Pacific (4–6–2) Winston Churchill, one of ten locomotives running on the $15\frac{1}{8}$ in. gauge track of the Romney, Hythe and Dymchurch Light Railway in Kent.

Over a hollow sub-structure, such as one made by any of the methods just described, a firm crust or skin has to be formed that will represent the actual surface of the ground. There are several different materials that can be used satisfactorily as a basis for this. Wire mesh, perforated metal gauze and expanded metal are often chosen. Hessian or sacking soaked in or daubed liberally with plaster or household filling compound is sometimes used. In one of the quickest and cheapest methods a crust or skin composed principally of newspaper is built up. The newspaper is first torn into pieces about the size of a man's hand. These are then soaked in wallpaper paste, or the paste is brushed over them generously. Then they are placed over the supporting structure so that they cover and hide it. Up to three layers of pasted paper can be applied at one time. After that, it is best if they are left to dry out thoroughly before more layers are added.

Even before the ground surface is complete and dry the modeller will have been thinking about the texture of every part of it. Normally, in temperate countries, grass will grow on almost every fertile surface, and fortunately for modellers it can be imitated quite easily – the method used being usually determined by the gauge of the railway (even the blades in the tufts of grass should be correct to scale, some would say!). Medical lint is popular with many modellers. Others prefer a less smooth and even surface, and use this technique: on to a freshly painted surface, dyed sawdust or rayon flock is scattered. When the paint is dry, the surplus sawdust or flock is blown or brushed lightly away, leaving the rest adhering to the surface. To produce subtleties of colour the grass can be given one or more coats of water paint or it can be sprayed with one of the matt colours specially produced for model-makers.

Cultivated soil can be represented almost as easily as grass – with paper tissue smeared with a generous application of wallpaper paste. The wet tissue can be formed into furrows, or crinkles, or any other desired texture. The surface which results when the paste is dry can be painted with matt colour so that it resembles natural earth.

Small stones or pebbles can be used to represent rocks, and boulders and larger rock surfaces can be built up with plaster, or by using cork bark, or the bark from almost any other dead tree. Usually the indentations will represent the strata of rock formations very convincingly.

Road surfaces have to be made with care if the roads in a miniature landscape are not to look less realistic than the railway tracks they run beside (or cross). Roads that are quite flat rarely look convincing – unless a backward country district is serving as the prototype – since most modern roads have a distinct camber. Good road surfaces can be given a true colour and texture with a mixture

Lord Gretton has a mile-long 10¼ in. gauge miniature railway at Stapleford park, Leicestershire. On the turn-table is the Stapleford Miniature Railway John of Gaunt, a free lance Atlantic (4–4–2) locomotive built by David Curwen about 1950. This particular locomotive featured in one of the episodes in the television series 'The Avengers'

185 Above – Squawbottom is the lowest point of the Gorre and Daphetid layout. The scenery at this point extends from floor to ceiling.

186 Left – The high steel trestle bridge at Grand Cliff in John Allen's layout was made of wood and card.

187 Above, right – Part of Whitney K. Towers' Alturas and Lone Pine layout, showing the superb juxtaposition of buildings and landscape.

188 Right – Another view of the Alturas and Lone Pine layout with the foreground merging beautifully with the back cloth.

of grey paint and sand or coal dust. Country lanes and tracks can be surfaced with a mixture of paint and the ballast or small stones used with the railway track – the colour of the paint being chosen to echo the colour of the local earth. Modellers who wish to be historically accurate often have to find out the date of the introduction of modern road-surfacing materials into the regions they are using as prototypes.

Plants, shrubs and other natural forms that grow on or above the ground call for much skill and ingenuity on the part of the model-maker. Trees, especially, can badly let down the rest of a railway layout. All model trees should look as if they have grown out of the ground and have not been just placed on it or fixed into it, and this is not easy to manage. Commercially made plastic trees of many different sorts and sizes are now on sale in most countries and some look reasonably lifelike, but model-makers who set the highest standards of realism usually prefer to make their own.

The best method involves the use of many lengths of copper or some other flexible wire. These are bound together over one part of their length to form the tree trunk, and then the strands are separated on each side of this to form the roots and branches. Paper tissue, coated with paste, is wrapped round the trunk and main branches, to represent the bark – which it does very well, forming surprisingly natural wrinkles and serrations. The wood is afterwards painted with matt paint in suitable colours.

There are many ways in which foliage can be represented. The

189 Even in the compact space of a Minitrix layout, scenery can be constructed which does not strain the viewer's credulity.

most careful modellers look for the method that is most appropriate for each kind of tree. Foam plastic, torn or shredded to look like leaves and soaked with dye or paint is often used, and so are dried tea leaves, dried moss and lichen, sprinkled with sawdust, and the material known as horsehair packing or rubberized hair. For the foliage of some fruit trees, one of the world's most successful model-makers used to recommend millet spray – the branches left in a stripped state by hungry cage birds being, he found, especially realistic. Unfortunately, this may have only a limited life.

Bushes and hedges are not so difficult to represent in miniature. They can be made from foam rubber, moss, lichen, or any other material that can be trimmed or torn to a suitable shape and fixed with adhesive in the required position. A tiny box hedge in one of the layouts at Pendon is made from a special kind of surgical rubber normally used for the treatment of varicose ulcers.

Water is difficult to incorporate successfully in a miniature landscape, attractive as tiny lakes and rivers and waterfalls may be. If the water is left to stand about without moving it is liable to become dusty and unpleasant. If it is encouraged to circulate by mechanical means it can create moist conditions unsuitable for small engines that are better kept dry. Most modellers prefer to use, as a safe and inert substitute, a sheet of clear glass, or a piece of cellophane that has been crumpled to simulate ripples, or even a piece of the dimpled glass made specially for bathrooms and other private places. A shallow depression can be formed quite easily

190 Very realistic alpine scenery has been modelled for the Gauge IO Swissminiatur layout.

91 *Above, left — Sutter Creek on the Alturas and Lone Pine layout showing the perfect positioning of the bridge and tunnel entrances.*

92 *Left — Realistically represented mountains on the Italian State Railways layout of W. A. Corkill. The bridge is from Kibri.*

93 *Right, above — A view of part of a layout that shows an enlarged photograph for the background*

94 *Right, centre — English hill scenery in a layout of the London Midland and Scottish Railway.*

95 *Right, below — New Zealand landscape on R. H. Stott's layout of the Taputerangi Timber Co.'s branch tramway.*

in the ground of a model landscape so that it will represent the bed of a river or lake. Then, it can be painted with suitable colours and planted with artificial water-weeds before it is given a water-to-air surface with one of these transparent or translucent materials. This will produce a remarkably liquid effect. So, too, will the application of several coats of clear varnish to a carefully modelled river bed.

There are few model railway layouts of any size that do not include at least one tunnel – tunnels are popular with modellers because they allow trains to be withdrawn temporarily from public view. They provide a certain extra element of romance, too, since from the earliest days of railways tunnels have been regarded as perilous places – understandably, since an accident in a dark, confined place where rescue work is difficult or even impossible must seem especially terrible. In model railway systems, the hazards of tunnels are reduced in due proportion to their size. The worst accidents occur when kittens and other small pets choose these convenient, untenanted burrows as secluded places for sleep.

The catalogue of features that might properly be considered under the general heading of landscape could be extended almost indefinitely – even, possibly, as far as details as irrelevant but amusing as the small birds that alight and perch temporarily on the trackside telegraph wires, faithfully reproduced in the meticulously modelled set-pieces of Norm Gaby, of Hamilton, New Zealand – but it must be kept within limits.

It would be wrong to close the list, though, without remembering line-side signs. These are to be found in an almost unclassifiable variety in all parts of the world where railways run. If they are reproduced with care, so that the lettering is of exactly the same kind as that on the originals, and to scale, they may play a big part in establishing the authenticity of a railway landscape. Besides the boards that bear such imperative messages as NO TRESPASSING, BEWARE OF THE TRAINS, WHISTLE and WARNING: KEEP OFF

196 A model of a railcar in the New Zealand bush. The trees have been particularly well portrayed by R. H. Stott.

ELECTRIC LIVE RAILS, there are also the less obvious, but to the perceptive observer no less significant, operational signs found in most systems, such as the gradient posts erected historically where-ever there was a change of gradient in the line, or the coasting boards that tell the driver of an electrically operated train when to shut off his power supply so that he may coast economically into a station.

And, one should not forget miniature figures, even if, like many modellers, one feels that a landscape bristling with motionless people – some of them frozen, perhaps, in strange attitudes – is less full of life than a landscape with no humans in it at all.

Most of the great commercial companies have made and sold single figures, and sets of figures, intended to add a little extra interest to their model stations and other buildings. (Wenman Bassett-Lowke's most memorable venture in this direction was a set of celebrity passengers – recognizable portraits, or caricatures, of famous people, reduced, like all his best work, exactly to scale. The set included one figure that many people took to be a miniature replica of Wenman Bassett-Lowke himself.) But these, as they must be, have all been lifeless.

An ingenious novelty is to be seen in an entertaining exhibition layout devised by the British modeller Jack Dugdale. It involves the use of two photo-electric cells, three relay coils, and a power supply. With their aid, a small figure – that of a ganger inspecting the track – is actually made to move, and at an appropriate time. As a train approaches the section of the line on which the ganger is working, it breaks a light beam, and the ganger jumps smartly back out of danger. When the train has passed, it breaks a second light beam, further along the line, and the ganger jumps forward again, ready to resume his work!

It is not surprising that, of all the model railway layouts in which particular attention is given to the landscape, the most impressive should be those in which mountainous terrain is represented successfully. John Allen's Gorre and Daphetid layout, described in Chapter 10, owes much of its grandeur to the lofty peaks and steep-sided canyons that (most naturalistically) threaten to dwarf the Wizard of Monterey's little trains. W. A. Corkill, a business man from Cheshire, England, has set most of his layout in the Dolomites. The excellent layout known as Swissminiatur, at Meilide, near Lugano, is possibly the best-known model railway system in Europe with a high-altitude setting. Here, the whole layout is to scale, as all good layouts should be – with the exception of the mountains. If these miniature replicas of the neighbouring Alps had been carried out in their true proportions, they would have had to be made more than four hundred feet high. For a model railway layout, this was asking rather a lot.

15 Outdoor and Garden Railways

A model railway enthusiast has said 'It is, I believe, the ambition of many people today to possess two cars' (that is, automobiles). 'Mine has been to possess two railways, one indoors, one in the garden.'

It is easy to understand this man's yearning for alternative ways of satisfying his creative urges. When the weather is fine and warm, it seems – to many people – a waste of one of the greatest blessings life can send, to stay in any enclosed place. When weather conditions are unfavourable for outdoor work, a modeller with a garden railway and no indoor layout can only feel frustrated. There are no published figures to support this contention, but it is safe to say that the relationship between the number of indoor and outdoor model railway layouts in any country depends to a large extent on its climatic conditions. In a land where the hours of sunshine are likely to be pleasantly prolonged, where temperatures are not too extreme and heavy rainfall and strong winds are almost unknown there are likely to be more outdoor layouts in use than there are in, for example, the whole of clammy Britain, or in the countries of the far north with their inhibiting periods of twilight and darkness.

There is, of course, a compromise solution to the problems set by a preponderantly depressing climate, and that is for each perplexed enthusiast to make for himself a dual-purpose layout that is provided with adequate shelter – it may have the greater part of its permanent way in a garden, perhaps, and the passenger and freight yards in a shed.

Even more ambitious is the practice of linking a self-contained indoor layout with a garden line.

This is not practicable, for obvious reasons, where the indoor part of such a layout would be on an appreciably different level form the outdoor part – as, for example, if it were in a cellar or on an upper floor. Where an indoor layout has been made on the ground floor, the construction of a tunnel through the outer wall of the building is a relatively simple matter. Then, if the track is organized on an out-and-home plan, so that the line loops back on itself, the operator can dispatch his trains on round-the-garden

97 D. H. Neale's magnificent mm. scale garden railway. The Deeley Viaduct needed 2,800 lb. f concrete.

journeys from the comparative comfort of his living room –
watching their progress, possibly, from an ordinary domestic
window until they return again, through the tunnel, to the warm
and sheltered hearth.

The modeller who decides to make an outdoor or partly outdoor
layout has to overcome certain difficulties that do not trouble the
man who works in a dry, well ventilated, pleasantly heated room.
Exposed to the full rigors of the weather, model railway track is
liable to oxydize quickly (tinplate, which will start to rust in a
single afternoon if it gets wet, is obviously unsuitable). So, the
wise outdoor or garden specialist sees that his track is particularly
well drained. Ballast, for a garden line in all but the driest climates,
has to consist of some hard, coarse granular material such as
granite chippings or flint chicken grit. (Chicken grit made from
crushed shells will not do. The dust that blows up from this can be
guaranteed to wreck any normal mechanism!) Ties or sleepers
that are made of wood have to be treated regularly with creosote or
some other preservative. Track made with plastic ties that are
virtually weather-proof is especially suitable for outdoor use.

Many small outdoor railways are designed to carry live passengers, and the locomotives on these lines are usually powered by
live steam. Where the primary intention of the operator is to give

*198 Two New Zealand M class
locomotives in Gauge O, built by
Frank Roberts around old Hornby
electric motors. They are seen
running over an outdoor viaduct.*

pleasure to as many people as possible, by taking them for rides, it is a waste of time to aim at a high degree of realism. Inevitably, any human being, even a child, will look ridiculously out of scale when making a journey on a miniature train drawn by an engine that is no larger – and may even be appreciably smaller – than any of the passengers. In these circumstances, it is usually found best to raise the track well above the ground, on trestles or some other supports, so that the legs of the travellers can hang down comfortably below track-level, on either side.

Outdoor model railways are made, now, in most gauges from N upward, layouts with track made to 5 inch gauge and $7\frac{1}{4}$ inch gauge being especially popular. Where gauges larger than 12 inch are chosen, the layouts and the stock that run on them cannot properly be called models and so are really outside the scope of this book. Be that as it may, the words model railway still conjure up in the minds of many people the delightful miniature systems designed and made by Wenman Bassett-Lowke's company, for use in public parks and at seaside resorts; his garden railways, made for Sir Robert Walker, Sir Edward Nicholl, Captain Holder, and other well-to-do clients; and – possibly the most famous outdoor miniature system of all – the Romney, Hythe and Dymchurch Light Railway, that operates on a fourteen mile stretch of the British south coast.

*199 A French outdoor LGB model
train in scale 1 to 22.5 in M.
Fournereau's collection.*

The Romney, Hythe and Dymchurch Light Railway had its origins, like so many other layouts, in the dreams and aspirations of a single man – in this case, the creative genius was a Captain John Howey. The chief centre of interest in Captain Howey's original 15 inch gauge garden layout was his celebrated 4–6–2 three ton locomotive called, fittingly, *Colossus*. This engine, which was more than eighteen feet long, was powerful enough to haul a train with two hundred passengers.

Shortly after the end of the First World War, the directors of the English Southern Railway Company were considering whether they should operate a standard (4 feet 8½ inches) gauge extension line in the district. Instead of doing so, however, they approached Captain Howey, whose personal railway was by that time well known, and they asked him if he would care to build and operate a public passenger-carrying line that would be a development of the small private system he was already operating so successfully. The Captain agreed, and before long eight miles of track had been laid – the length of the main railway being extended, later, to nearly fourteen miles, and, with subsidiary lines, to twenty-seven.

200 Left – A raised outdoor railway under construction in a woodland setting. This is mixed gauge : 3½ in. and 5 in. The rails are in aluminium alloy and the sleepers are of hardwood.

201 Right – Switches for an outdoor miniature railway being inspected before being transported to the site. This track too is mixed gauge : 7¼ in. and 10¼ in. The angle of the crossing is 1 in 7¼.

202 *Typical of many modern miniature railways, this is a 10¼ in. gauge 'Western' class diesel locomotive pulling articulated trucks (cars). It is powered by a Ford 1,600 c.c. cross-flow engine.*

The new miniature line was an immediate success, and attracted many thousands of visitors each year to that part of the coast. It is still being operated – more than 360,000 passengers were carried on it during 1968. And, it is now one of the few public railways in Great Britain that runs at a reasonable profit!

Among the countries that have climates particularly suitable for outdoor work are New Zealand and South Africa.

The emphasis on outdoor work in New Zealand may stem, at least in part, from the pioneering example of the late Frank Roberts, a retired locomotive driver, who, with his friend W. W. Stewart, first put his country on the railway modelling map. Roberts' Gauge 1 models, based largely on New Zealand Railway prototypes and exquisitely detailed, are now carefully preserved by the Publicity Section of the New Zealand Railways Department as memorials to his prodigious labours. One of the outstanding outdoor layouts in more recent years has been that owned and operated by Maurice Duston, one of the leading lights of the New Zealand Model Railway Association, and a great admirer of Frank Roberts' work. Mr Duston's layout has been a popular meeting place for members of the Association, many of whom have gone away at the close of each session determined to construct outdoor layouts of their own.

In South Africa, many model engineers are also busily engaged in making and operating miniature railway systems. There is (to take only one example) a 10¼ inch gauge line on a beach on the Simonstown side of the Cape Peninsula. Based on South African practice, it has a fine freelance 4–6–2 live steam locomotive that handles long rakes of coaches with impressive ease.

Mexico has at least one outdoor light railway, and there are several in the United States of America.

The Australian equivalent of the Romney, Hythe and Dymchurch Light Railway is the Puffing Billy – the only remaining example of four narrow gauge lines that were built by the Victorian Government at the beginning of this century. For fifty years this diminutive train served the local community by hauling passengers and freight along a winding, 18 mile long track between Upper Ferntree Gully and Gembrook in the Dandenong Ranges near Melbourne. During those years the little train with its fussy steam engines and quaint rolling stock endeared itself to the people of Victoria, so that when the line was closed, officially, in 1954, because of heavy financial losses resulting in part from a landslide that had covered the tracks in the previous year, the residents of Melbourne formed the Puffing Billy Preservation Society. The work of this society has made it possible for Puffing Billy to remain in existence – no longer as a freight train, but as one of Victoria's greatest tourist attractions.

16 Operation

The many excellent histories that have been written of the early railways make gruesome reading. How ever, one wonders, did any travellers who trusted themselves to these happy-go-lucky enterprises manage to survive?

There were so many other hazards, besides cows and horses. People like the pompous charlatan Doctor Dionysius Lardner, for instance, who in 1838 managed to persuade the directors of a well-known railway company that he was an expert, and wished to carry out research that they would find valuable. Taken in by the Doctor's unceasing flow of pseudo-scientific terms, the railwaymen lent him an experimental train and gave him the freedom of their lines. For eight glorious weeks, the Doctor's train roamed at will over their system, to the immediate peril of all using the regular services. The great Daniel Gooch himself wrote in his diary:

> 'When I look back upon this time, it is a marvel to me that we escaped serious accidents. It was no uncommon thing to take an engine out on the line to look for a late train that was expected, and many times have I seen the train coming and reversed the engine and run back out of its way as quickly as I could. What would be said of such a proceeding now?'

Today, trains travel safely across continents at speeds that are more than six times as fast as those ever reached by Robert Stephenson's *Rocket*. They are able to do so, because the principles on which railways are operated have been studied as carefully and have stimulated as many brilliant ideas as those that govern the design of high-powered locomotives. It is not surprising that some railway modellers are rather less interested in the appearance of their models than they are in the completely reliable and controlled way in which their models work.

Dependable working, then, is the basis of the strange, esoteric activity known in the railway modelling world as operation. (One of the classic stories told by modellers is that of the American soldier who, called away to do his duty in a certain struggle in Korea, spent his last hours before embarkation *playing* with his model *rail-*

203 The control panel for the freight yards in a Gauge OO layout.

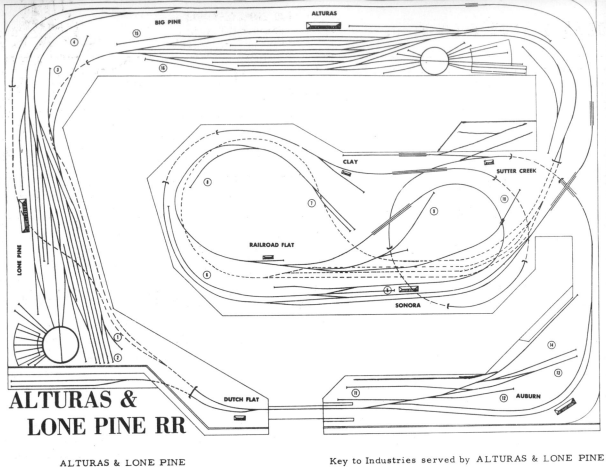

ALTURAS & LONE PINE RR

ALTURAS & LONE PINE
"Vital Statistics"

Room size: 22' x 26'; 572 square feet.
Railroad size (excluding aisles); 350 sq. ft.
Total Trackage: 600 linear feet.
Length of Mainline: 170 linear feet.
Length of Branchline: 30 linear feet.
Length of Yards and Spurs: 400 linear feet.
Average length Passing Sidings: 12 feet.
Maximum Mainline Grade: 3% uncompensated.
Minimum Mainline Curve: 30 inch radius.
Control: 2 Engineer Cabs; 4 Tower Panels.
100 Turnouts, controlled by rotary switch machines.
All Turnouts either #6 or #8.
Equipment: ALP: 25 Steam Locomotives
            TLC: 2 Steam Locomotives
            WP: 5 Diesel Locomotives
            ALP: 175 Freight Cars
                  20 Passenger Cars
                  12 Cabooses

Key to Industries served by ALTURAS & LONE PINE

(1) Kraus Oil Co. wholesale oil distributors
(2) Whit's Wood Works, wood products
(3) Northside Tool Co. machine shop
(4) Century Furniture Mfg. Co.
(5) Team Track
(6) Trojan Logging Co. Interchange Track
(7) Radebaugh Drilling Co. crude oil producers
(8) Burdick's Better Bulls, cattle
(9) Trojan Logging Co. lumber mill
(10) Keeling Mine, coal mine
(11) Robinson's Foundry, metal fabricators
(12) Linn-Mill Feed & Grain, warehouse
(13) Walsh's Warehouse, general merchandise
(14) McClanahan Refining Company
(15) Bulline Packers, meat packing
(16) Icing Platform, reefer stage icing

These are industries as of January 1, 1962, but more
are under construction. W A T C H   U S   G R O W !

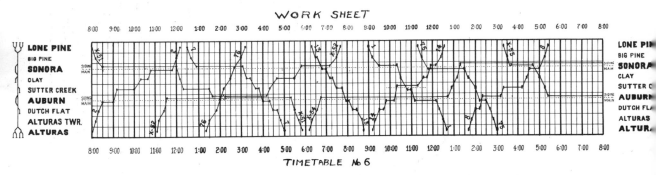

WORK SHEET

TIMETABLE № 6

...TURAS & LONE PINE R. R.

Time-Table No.

NORTHWARD							READ DOWN		MILES	STATIONS	CALL LETTERS	SIDING CAPACITY	SOUTHWARD								READ UP	
7	7	X-51	13	1	75	1	75	X-53					2	X-52	2	76	X-52	X-54	X-52	14	X-54	8
1ST Class			1ST Class WOODS-MAN	1ST Class ALP FLYER	2ND Class			3RD Class					1ST Class ALP FLYER	3RD Class		2ND Class		3RD Class		1ST Class WOODS-MAN		1ST C
Passenger			Passenger	Passenger				Local Freight					Passenger	Local Freight		Thru Reefer		Local Freight		Passenger		Pass
PM	PM	PM	PM	PM	PM		AM	AM					AM	AM	AM	AM	PM	PM	PM	AM	AM	A
12:30			6:20	9:00	11:20			A-53 MU-5 3:20	0.0	LONE PINE	LP	60		T-1 12:10	T-5 3:10					T-PA BD 7:40	T-PA ⑥ 12:35	T-7
12:40			6:30 6:35	9:10	11:30		3:30		4.0	BIG PINE	BP	15		12:00	3:00					7:30	12:25	
12:55	3:05	→ SO-HE PU-HE	6:50 7:00	S 9:30 1020	M 11:50		1:30	MSS 3:45 SO-5 4:40 ⑤	9.5	SONORA	S	14	SO-D → 10:50	11:50 →	2:40	SO-5 PU-5 5:50			7:10 M S	12:10 1155	SO-5 ⑤ 1:20 M
	3:15 3:25		7:10 7:20	10:30			1:40	5:00	14.3	CLAY	C	4	10:40 10:20		2:30	SO-1 5:30 PU-1 4:40				1145 1135	1:10
X-51	3:40 3:50		7:30 7:45	M 10:50 11:00			2:00	5:15	19.7	SUTTER CREEK	SC	8	PU-D 10:00 9:10		2:10		4:20		M S	11:20 1020	12:55	
→ PU-5 1:40 ⑤	4:00 4:20	→ 5:20	7:55 8:05	SO-D 11:10		→ 12:10	M 2:10 2:30	SO-5 PU-5 5:25	22.5	AUBURN	AU	25	9:00 8:30	SO-5 PU-5 1135 ⑤	2:00		4:10 PU-5 6:45 ⑤			1010 9:50	12:45 M	→ PU-5
	4:30 4:40		8:15 8:25			12:20		2:40	25.8	DUTCH FLAT	DF	20	8:20	11:25			1:50	6:35		940 930		
	4:50	5:40	8:40			12:30		2:50	31.1	ALTURAS TWR	AT	0	8:10	11:10			1:30	6:20		920		
T-8 5:00 BD	T-PA 5:50	T-14 8:45				T-2 12:40		T-PA I-T-E 3:00	33.5	ALTURAS	A	60	8:01	11:05		A-76 T-F-E 1:20		A-54 MU 6:10		A-14 9:10	
PM	PM	PM	PM	PM	PM		AM	AM					AM	AM	AM	AM	PM	PM	PM	AM	AM	

GENERAL RULES

TRAINS are superior by direction to east bound trains.

LASS TRAINS hold main unless otherwise instructed.
TRAINS take siding unless otherwise instructed.

OUT signifies A.M.
ON (GREEN) signifies P.M.

BLR INDICATIONS
Passenger (Diesel or steam powered)
Passenger (Gas Electric)
4-car freight
5-car freight
6-car freight
Through freight

INDICIA
over
ayover
ate Run

or cab control 15 minutes before scheduled train times.

REFERENCE LETTERS

A **ASSEMBLE** followed by TRAIN NO. next train using same equipment.

I **INTERCHANGE** – may be followed by:
  E   Exchange cars with others within yard limits.
  F   From Western Pacific
  T   To Western Pacific

M **MEET**

S **TAKE SIDING**

T **TURN** (loco and rear car) – may be followed by
  C   Combine   E   Exchange cars with others
  PA   Put Away   within yard limits.
  TRAIN NO. next train using same equipment.

BD **BREAK DOWN** train and spot cars at local industries.

MU **MAKE UP** from cars at local industries.

PU **PICK UP** } followed by { # Number of cars.
SO **SET OUT** }   { D Diner
                { HE Head end car.

REFERENCE NUMBERS

① Limit train to 8 cars maximum.

② Spot on "Hold" track.

③ Prior to 10:50 A.M., back to south end of siding (Block

④ Work No. 53 before No. 54.

⑤ Immediately after No. 76 passes, reverse position of N
    and No. 52 on siding, using main line for runarou

⑥ Hold in Block 4A for arrival of No. 51 north.

⑦ Run by on main line and back in on siding (Block 8A).

204 The Alturas and Lone Pine
Railroad. The diagrams on these
two pages show something of the
complexity of operations carried
out by Whitney K. Towers on his
layout. Above, left, a plan; left,
he work sheet for timetable
No. 6; above, right, timetable
No. 6; and right, a local timetable.

ALTURAS & LONE PINE R.R.   LOCAL TIMETABLE 6

SOUTHBOUND				TIME			NORTHBOUND	
TRAIN NO.	NAME OR KIND		ARR. LVE. CLAY	PASS SONORA	AM PM BIG PINE		NAME OR KIND	TRAIN NO.
				SO-5 PU-5 ③ 8:30	8:10 ←		LOCAL FREIGHT	X-51
2	ALP FLYER →		10:20 10:40	SO-D 10:50 11:50	12:00			X 51
			12:10	12:01 ←				
				SO-HE PU-HE S (M) 12:55	1240 ←		PASS-ENGER	7
76	THRU REEFER →		2:30	(M) 2:40	3:00			7
			3:15 3:25	3:05 ←				
X-52	LOCAL FREIGHT		4:40 5:30	SO-5 PU-5 5:50				
			7:10 7:20	6:50 7:00	6:30 6:35 ←		WOODS-MAN	13
X 52	→			7:10	7:30			
			10:30	PU-D S 9:30 1020	8:10 ←		ALP FLYER	1
				(M) 11:50	11:30 ←		THRU REEFER	75
14	WOODS-MAN →		11:35 11:45	M S 11:55 12:10	12:25			
X 54	LOCAL FREIGHT →		1:10	SO-5 PU-5 1:20				
			1:40	1:30 →	←			75
8	PASS-ENGER →			SO-5 PU-5 S ⑦ 3:45 (M) ④	3:30 ←		LOCAL FREIGHT	X-53
			4:25	(M) 4:35 5:00	5:15			
			5:00	4:40 →	←			X 53

roads. When, some dirty and bloody years later, he returned from the distant battlefields he gave those nearest and dearest to him the embraces they, after such a long, long separation, reasonably expected from him. Then, as soon as he could legitimately detach himself from them, he dashed upstairs to his model railroad. On the track, there was a tiny train – so it is said – still obstinately plugging its way round on the journey he had plotted for it before he went off to the wars. That, in a nutshell, is what is meant by the magical word performance.)

So, performance is the factor without which one cannot start to think about operation. But though one is dependent on the other, the two things are entirely different. Operation, as strictly defined by the magazine *Model Railroader*, 'has to do with train scheduling, routing and car distribution, not engine or car running qualities.'

The senior members of the great railway modellers' associations have wisely recognized that the general public is not interested in operation in the strictest sense of the term. People flock dutifully to exhibition layouts, and they pay to see them, so these layouts must appear to work. But the organizers know that most of the people who crowd in at the turnstiles are not at all interested in the sort of activities that really make a model railway railway-like – station work, train-marshalling, time-table operation, and mentally demanding occupations like that. All most people want to see is trains in motion – and the more trains there are in motion, the happier they become. So, the old argument about whether a layout should be continuous or point-to-point does not often arise in the context of public exhibitions. In these rather special circumstances it is generally agreed that a layout that allows continuous running will serve its purpose best.

Having taken this decision almost automatically, the people who put on the shows know that they can expect certain inevitable advantages.

First, they can be confident that all but the most exacting of their spectators will be satisfied. The operation of an end-to-end layout entails a great deal of stopping and starting, which can be boring to the uninitiated. On a continuous layout, there need be few interruptions.

Then, they will not find it quite so hard to enroll assistants who are willing to operate a system of this type and who are capable of doing it without exposing the organization to public shame. Almost any keen but comparatively unskilled operator who is disengaged during exhibition hours can run a continuous line which does not require elaborate shunting.

The third advantage brings us back again to performance. Any continuous layout that is to be operated can usually have a substantial part of its track concealed from the general view behind hardboard mountains or some other carefully arranged screens. This allows a lot of the necessary maintenance work to be carried out in private while the railway is running – there is so much dirt and dust around in most public assembly rooms that regular inspections of the rolling stock, and cleaning, are essential. Often, too, a hidden soldering iron will prove useful for effecting emergency repairs.

But this is elementary stuff. The most advanced model railway operators usually prefer to work hidden from people who are less knowledgeable than themselves. One factor alone would make the doings of these clever people unintelligible to the casual passer-by: they are working in *scale time*. The hours, minutes and seconds that control the actions of all the rest of the world are not truly in proportion to the other elements in any ideal model railway layout until they have been suitably converted.

As long ago as 1930, a man called E. G. Mitton realised that railway models made to scale dimensions, running over distances that had been calculated exactly to scale, could be really convincing only if they were operated according to proportionately reduced times. In the first, heady excitement of his discovery, Mr. Mitton doctored a small alarm clock so that it gained twelve minutes during every one of the minutes that it had been accustomed to recording before. His action, intuitive rather than scientific, has been derided by later, more coldly rational experts, but as far as model railway operation is concerned it was one of the most important steps that have ever been taken into the unknown.

Soon, a basic principle of scale-time working became apparent – the ratio of scale time to real time cannot be selected arbitrarily, it must be individually tailored in every case to suit the particular type and size of railway. To take one outstandingly successful example – John Allen's Gorre and Daphetid layout, in Monterey, California, is operated on a scale-time ratio of 15 : 1 which distils a whole twelve-hour real-time working day into forty-eight minutes of concentrated excitement. This ratio, in which each scale or running minute is represented by four seconds of real time, was evolved only after lengthy consideration of train lengths and train weights, the performance of various locomotives, and the time taken to perform such necessary movements as coupling and uncoupling, loading and unloading, and so on. Anyone fortunate enough to be invited to assist with the operation of John Allen's layout will know exactly how earlier railroad operatives must have felt when they were faced with such challenging difficulties as four per cent gradients, trains loaded beyond their proper capacity, crippling track restrictions, and timetables tailored so exactly that working to them was a great test of nerve and stamina for everyone concerned.

Another famous American model railroad that is operated to strictly controlled time scale is the Alturas and Lone Pine, over which Whit Towers, currently a leading official of the National Model Railroad Association, presides.

The Alturas and Lone Railroad represents a prototype founded in 1858 to serve the mining communities of California's Mother Lode country. The men responsible for the original line arrived ten years too late to make their fortunes in the California Gold Rush, but they were quick to see the need for a dependable form of transport through the gold district that extends north and south along the foothills of the Sierra Nevada. Now, mining activity in the area has dwindled, but the line serves a wide variety of other interests – lumber and petroleum products, ranching, agriculture and general merchandising provide plenty of business still for the Alturas and Lone Pine line. Passenger traffic has remained relatively stable over the years, too, since the mountainous nature of the landscape did not encourage the rapid development of roads and highways. There is, then, on this railroad a nice balance between different kinds of traffic, and this makes it – in model form – especially interesting to operate.

A visitor to Mr Towers' home who is invited to act as a temporary member of the railroad company will work as one of a team. He may be allowed – to take a typical example – to run a fast freight train in a northward direction from Lone Pine to Alturas, where there is an interchange point with the Western Pacific Railway. The train will be made up or marshalled for him by the acting yardmaster. He – the yardmaster – will work from a specially prepared Switch List. This will tell him which cars are to be included in the train and the order in which they are to be arranged. It will show him, too, exactly where the cars are located before he starts to collect them, and it will indicate the ultimate destination of each. The letters and symbols used in the list will be exactly like those found in a prototype schedule.

By the time the yardmaster has done his job, the visitor will have

205 A commercial model of a track-diagram control panel composed of units which can be assembled in any sequence. This system can be used on any layout.

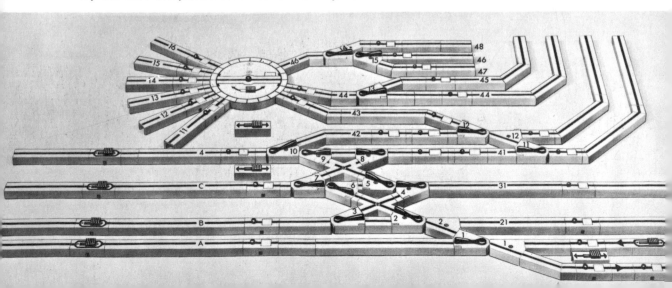

settled at the control panel from which he is to operate the train. Like all the electrical control panels on the Alturas and Lone Pine Railroad (model version) this is housed in a sliding drawer which can be pushed back into the benchwork, to provide extra aisle space, when it is not in use.

Before the freight train's journey can start, the operator must study the Train Order that has been made out, as in prototype systems, to give him his working instructions. This Train Order is a single-sheet printed form that has been filled in to show a schedule of departure and arrival times, together with lists of the cars that have to be dropped (set out) or picked up at each of the stations the train is to serve on its way. Copies of the Train Orders are given to the crew men responsible for these stations so that they can gather, in readiness, the cars that are to be picked up under their effective direction.

The operator must know, too, a few important facts about operation on the Alturas and Lone Pine Railroad – facts he can get from the 16-page heavy-cover *Alturas and Lone Pine Employee Time Table* – a book containing the overall instructions and house rules that apply to this carefully organized but genially adminstered system. He must know, for example, that he will be expected to keep as exactly as he can to his departure and arrival time schedule, using a scale-time clock which operates at a 12 : 1 ratio (that is, 60 scale minutes on the Alturas and Lone Pine prototype railroad are represented by 5 real minutes on the model). If he allows the train to fall more than five scale minutes behind schedule, he is expected to notify by telephone the member of the operating team who is acting as dispatcher.

To control the speed of his train, an operator on the Alturas and Lone Pine Railroad (model version) can choose between a Variac adjustable transformer and a transistorized momentum throttle. The latter allows gradual stops and starts and gives a particularly realistic representation of engine performance, so that the handler using it really gets the feel of handling a prototype

206 For perfect model operation remote control equipment is necessary. One example is this double slip switch, with remote control, typical of today's products.

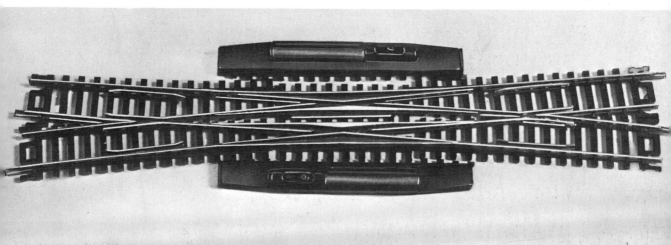

train. If, for instance, he shuts the throttle off suddenly, there is at first no apparent slackening of his train's speed —there would not be, in a real-life train, as the train's momentum would carry it on. Then, gradually, the model train slows down until eventually it stops. This slowing down and stopping process can take place over as much as a (scale) mile of track. To stop in a shorter distance, the operator may have to apply the brakes that are built into his control unit.

As a train moves along the main line at the Alturas and Lone Pine Railroad (model version) it passes a number of small posts. These are known by Whit Towers and his friends as Smile Posts. They are set up at the side of the track just as the prototype railroad has mile posts. The posts, in the model, are arranged at intervals of five (real) feet – that is, they are placed in approximately the same relationship to a scale mile (61 feet, in HO Gauge) as the scale time is to real time. The operator, watching his train pass the posts, can check its speed at a glance by referring to the time-speed charts provided in the Employee Time Table:

Time per Smile	mph	Volts (approx.)	Variac Setting (approx.)
1 min	60	12	85
1 min 20 sec	45	10	75
1 min 45 sec	35	8	70
2 min	30	7	65
3 min	25	6	55
4 min	15	5	45
6 min	10	4	35

The Smile Posts at Alturas and Lone Pine have a further function – they allow a main line journey of just under three miles (at the Gauge HO scale) to be stretched to 33.5 'smiles' – a piece of conjuring of which only the bigotted purists, with unlimited amounts of space for their own model railroads, could seriously disapprove.

So far, the task of acting as an engineer at a meticulously op-erated model railroad such as Alturas and Lone Pine may have appeared reasonably easy, but the man at the controls has some other responsibilities to shoulder, besides that of bringing his train to rest at its ultimate destination exactly at the scheduled time. As he is acting as the conductor or guard of the train, as well as its driver, he is responsible for its safety – and that means that he must look out for, and react to, all the customary signals. It means that if he is forced to make an unscheduled stop, he must protect his train with warning flags as called for by the book of Standard

Operating Rules. He must give the appropriate whistle signals, too, whenever his train approaches a highway or railroad crossing and when it reaches the limit of a yard.

An important task which is not normally included in the engineer's duties at Alturas and Lone Pine is that of dropping or setting out cars and of picking up others during the course of the journey. (It is done for him, there, by the yardmen.) This can only be carried out smoothly and efficiently if sufficient care has been taken, in the preliminary stages of making the railroad and equipping it with stock, with those small but vitally important details the couplers.

The invention of the first automatic coupling (and uncoupling) device was one of the most significant events in the history of model railway operation. Now, on any properly organized track, any engine can be backed up by remote control to any coach or car. As they meet, they become coupled together without being touched by hand, and they remain coupled together until the operator decides that they should separate. Car can be joined to car, or car to coach, with the same efficiency.

Unfortunately for the modeller who likes every part of his equipment to be exactly to scale, it is practically impossible to find an automatic coupler that is at the same time easy to operate, and reliable, and exactly like one particular prototype. There are a number of different designs which are more or less satisfactory compromises, but none can truly be said to conform to an international standard.

In one of the simplest and most popular systems, every locomotive, coach and goods wagon is fitted at each end with a coupler that consists of a fixed bar, and a moving hook with a striker below The hook and bar have been carefully shaped to ensure that when the coupler of another locomotive, coach or goods wagon approaches, the hook on the first coupler will touch the bar on the second coupler, and will pass over it, so that it grips the bar securely from the other side. Uncoupling can be carried out by raising spring-loaded ramps, or by raising ramps that are operated by electricity from a distance, or (as in the Rivarossi scheme) by passing the coupled vehicles over a magnet that will do the unlatching.

Before any model railway can be operated realistically, a lot of care has to be taken with those perennially difficult items of equipment, the switches. Switch operation can be roughly divided into three categories.

In the crudest type – appropriate only to layouts based on prototype railways that have not experienced the benefits (or otherwise) of modernization – the levers have to be changed or thrown manually. This is the cheapeast method of all to install, but there is

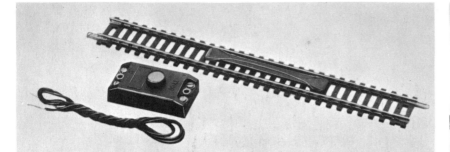

something a little disconcerting, if complete realism is being aimed at, in the sight of a large human hand with four large human fingers and a large thumb descending from the 'heavens' into a miniature layout that is otherwise perfectly to scale.

A little more closely adjusted to natural appearances are the more distant, mechanical methods of operation such as those in which the switch levers are thrown by means of lengths of piano wire concealed by, and running smoothly in, hollow flexible cables.

The most popular method of operating model railway switches is (as at the Alturas and Lone Pine Railroad) by remote electrical control. Most electric switch mechanisms are operated by means of solenoids, which are electro-magnets of a special type. Each solenoid consists of a coil of wire with a strip of ferrous metal inside it. The metal is separated from the coil, and can move freely, so that when an electric current is passed through the wire the strip moves with considerable force into the centre of the solenoid. To provide a simple push-pull movement, a pair of solenoids are normally used, one in front of the other, with a single metal strip running through both. When current is passed through the front solenoid, the bar is pulled forward. When it is passed through the the other solenoid, the bar is pulled back. Most electrically moti-

207 Above, top left – A remote control uncoupling set, comprising straight uncoupling track and control unit. This kind of equipment makes easier the realistic operation of model trains.

208 Above, left – A trackside ore bin and dump car operated by remote control.

209 Above – A power pack with speed and direction controls, having a reversing switch and a full range rheostat for all speeds.

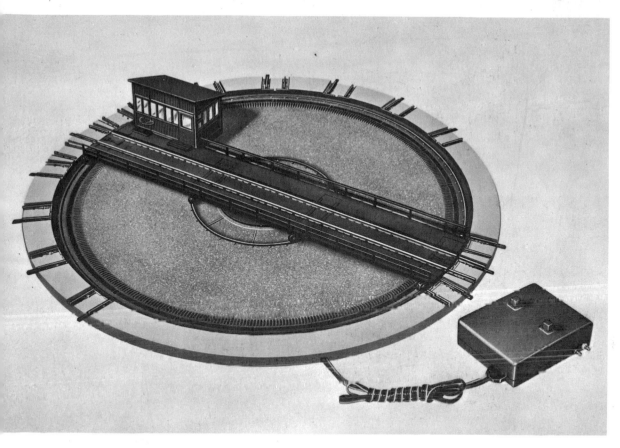

vated switches operate from 12 volts d.c. or 15 volts a.c., and take a
heavy current for a very short time. After they have done their job,
the current must be switched off, or they will rapidly become over-
heated. The replacement of burned-out coils may be one of the
larger expenses incurred by forgetful or heavy-handed owners in
the operation of their model railway layouts.

With so many instructions to bear in mind, so many signals to
watch for, an exact time schedule to work to, and a bewildering
number of buttons to press at exactly the right moment, a man
running a train on a great model railroad like Whit Towers' will be,
literally, taken out of himself. The 'two hours, forty minutes'
journey from Lone Pine to Alturas will have taken him, by the
watch on his wrist, a little less than a quarter of a real hour, and he
will have been as fully engrossed and occupied during that time
as if he had been running a real train on a real and important as-
signment. It is not surprising that men who in their working
hours bear heavy burdens of responsibility find that model railway operating, as a spare time occupation, makes a wonderful
distraction from routine cares. Some even change, for their hobby,
into true-to-prototype railway company uniforms, to make the
illusion complete.

For Further Reading

Boreham, D.A. *Narrow Gauge Railway Modelling.* Percival Marshall, London, 1962

Carter, E. F. *The Model Railway Encyclopaedia.* Burke, London, 1956

Carter, E. F. *The Railway Encyclopaedia.* Harold Starke, London, 1963

Day, J. R. *More Unusual Railways.* Frederick Muller, London, 1960

Day, J. R. with Cooper, B.K. *Railway Signalling Systems.* Frederick Muller, London, 1958

Day, J. R. with Cooper, B. K. *Railway Locomotives.* Frederick Muller, London, 1960

Day, J. R. with Wilson, B. G. *Unusual Railways.* Frederick Muller, London, 1958

Ellis, C. H. *British Railways History 1830–1876.* Allen and Unwin, London, 1956

Ellis, C. H. *British Railway History 1877–1947.* Allen and Unwin, London 1959

Ellis, C. H. *Model Railways 1839–1939.* Allen and Unwin, London, 1962

Evans, M. *Manual of Model Steam Locomotive Construction.* Model and Allied Publications, Hemel Hempstead, 1960

Hertz, L. H. *The Complete Book of Model Railroading.* Simmons-Boardman, New York, 1951

Hertz, L. H. *Collecting Model Trains.* Simmons-Boardman, New York, 1956

Jenkinson, D. and Campling, N. *Historic Carriage Drawings in 4 mm.* Ian Allan, Walton-on-Thames, 1969

Jenkinson, D. and Essery, R. J. *Locomotive Liveries of the L.M.S.* Ian Allan, Walton-on-Thames, 1967

Jenkinson, D. and Essery, R. J. *The L.M.S. Coach 1923–1957.* Ian Allan, Walton-on-Thames, 1969

'L.B.S.C.' *Simple Model Locomotive Building.* Model and Allied Publications, Hemel Hempstead, 1969

Morgan, B. *The Railway-Lover's Companion.* Eyre & Spottiswoode, London, 1963

Minns, J. E. *Model Railway Engines.* Weidenfeld and Nicolson, London, 1969

Nock, O. S. *The Railway Enthusiast's Encyclopedia.* Hutchinson, London, 1968

Ransome-Wallis, P. (Ed). *The Concise Encyclopedia of World Railway Locomotives.* Hawthorn, New York, 1959; Hutchinson, London, 1959

Rogers, Colonel H. C. B. *Turnpike to Iron Road,* Seeley Service, London, 1961

Rolt, L. T. C. *Red for Danger.* David and Charles, Newton Abbott, to be reprinted 1971

List of Illustrations

BLACK AND WHITE

Index

Figures in italic refer to illustration numbers